THE SIGNIFICANCE
OF THE CROSS

To E. M. D.

THE SIGNIFICANCE OF THE CROSS

by

F. W. DILLISTONE

Professor of Systematic Theology
Wycliffe College, Toronto

LUTTERWORTH PRESS
LONDON and REDHILL

PRINTED IN GREAT BRITAIN BY
LOWE AND BRYDONE PRINTERS LIMITED, LONDON, N.W.10

CONTENTS

PREFACE

In the spring of 1942 I was asked to give a course of lectures on " Preaching the Atonement " at the first School of Preaching at Wycliffe College, Toronto. This enabled me to put into shape certain ideas which had been developing in my mind. A few months later I used much of the same material when lecturing to the alumni of Huron College, London, Ontario. On each occasion, the response was exceedingly kind, and I was encouraged to put the lectures into more permanent form. There then followed a process of amplification and revision, in the course of which I was fortunate enough to have the interest and advice of my friend Professor R. J. McCracken, of McMaster University, Hamilton, Ontario, and at length a manuscript was ready for consideration. This again was expanded at the request of The Westminster Press, who had been good enough to accept it for publication, and the final work is now offered to a wider public.

For many years my chief interest theologically has been the doctrine of the Atonement. To two great writers I owe the sense of the centrality of the cross in Christian doctrine and I am deeply conscious of my indebtedness to them both. It could well be claimed that no greater Scottish theologian has arisen in this century than James Denney and no greater English theologian than P. T. Forsyth — and he was a Scot by birth! No writer has, I think, influenced my thought more than has Forsyth, and it is cause for much thanksgiving that he has at last come into his own. As far as the Biblical foundations of the doctrine are concerned, it will be obvious from the text how much I have learned from the recent writings of men like Vincent Taylor and Newton Flew and C. H. Dodd. Such writers

vii

have supplied an indispensable basis of historical investigation for anyone who would seek to construct a formulation of essential Christ doctrine.

The general plan of the book may be seen from the table of contents. There are two main sections, one devoted to an examination of the New Testament foundations of the doctrine, one to its reinterpretation in terms of present-day thoughts and ideas. The book should therefore move between the two poles of history and the imagination, for it is, I believe, within such a polar movement that the most satisfying results are to be obtained today. We cannot simply dwell in the exalted realm of the imagination; nor can we simply bury ourselves in a mass of historical detail. We need surely to go backwards and forwards between the two, ever seeking to relate historical facts imaginatively to the circumstances of the present time. Thus in relation to the doctrine of the Atonement our chief object must ever be to enter imaginatively into the meaning of the cross for every department of human life today, and that is what is attempted in the second part of the book; at the same time this can be done only by constant reference to the facts which are so faithfully and soberly recorded for us by the writers of the New Testament, and the attempt is made to examine these in the first half. It is to be hoped that the earlier part of the book will not appear to be too solid; if it does, it will certainly be offset by the second half, which may in places seem to be too light and too dependent upon transient ideas. The author would only ask the reader to co-operate with him by seeking to hold the two parts together and then to pass judgement on the book as a whole.

In conclusion, I have the pleasant task of expressing my thanks to various friends who have helped me more than perhaps they know. First I am deeply indebted to President John Alexander Mackay of Princeton and to Professor John Wick Bowman of Pittsburgh for their constant kindness and encour-

agement. Then I shall ever remember with gratitude the way
in which the Rev. L. J. Trinterud, of The Westminster Press,
has helped me by taking over the responsibility of publication
and by placing at my disposal his own wide knowledge and experience in this particular field. Finally I realize that the writing of this book was in large measure made possible by the
wonderfully happy conditions under which my normal labours
are carried on. The principal, staff, and students of Wycliffe
College have supplied in abundance that oil of fellowship
which helps to make life run smoothly and renders possible
the performance of certain tasks beyond the ordinary routine.
To them and to Miss Marion Taylor, of the College Office,
who has given me invaluable assistance by her skilful typing,
I tender my heartfelt thanks.

F. W. DILLISTONE

December, 1943.

1. The Cross Threads of the Web of Life

> *"As unknown, and yet well known; as dying, and, behold, we live; as chastened, and not killed; as sorrowful, yet alway rejoicing; as poor, yet making many rich; as having nothing, and yet possessing all things."*
>
> — *II Cor. 6:9, 10.*

Strange stories have been told from time to time of a cross appearing in the sky or printing itself upon the hands of a man. At such a time as this, however, there is no need to look for heavenly phenomena or to marvel at earthly stigmata; the whole range of human existence seems to lie under the shadow of the cross, and in whichever direction we turn we seem to find a situation in some way reminiscent of Calvary. Thus the title of this chapter, which is actually a chance phrase taken from a recent book of Stephen Leacock's, may well serve as an introduction to the general theme with which this book is concerned.

Almost instinctively we feel that this phrase gives an apt description of life as we know it. Life is not just a straight and unbroken thread, stretching from birth to death without tangles or cross patterns. On the contrary, we may examine life where we will and find conflicts and contrasts and even contradictions; no metaphor taken from smooth, one-way, unimpeded motion will serve. But how appropriate is the metaphor of the cross threads! If there is truth in the claim of the Time Spirit in Goethe's *Faust:*

> " Thus on the roaring loom of time I ply,
>   And weave for God the garment thou seest Him by,"

still more is it true that God is using the same loom to weave for man the pattern of his life here upon earth. A Scottish hymn writer has expressed this thought in her familiar lines:

" With mercy and with judgement
    My web of time He wove,"

but we might add to the threads of mercy and judgement those of joy and sorrow, of light and darkness, of exaltation and disappointment, of calm and anxiety, of success and failure, of hope and despair. " The Cross Threads of the Web of Life " is a phrase which can be tested by human experience and shown to be a true representation of reality.

But while the phrase provides an apt and telling metaphor of man's life as it actually is, there is something else about it which makes a subtle appeal to our minds. The very mention of the word ' cross ' in connection with the human scene brings up subconscious memories and associations which make us feel instinctively that the use of the word is right. In some curious way a cross has become a part of the very warp and woof of human existence. Often the texture of life has seemed disordered and confused, but gradually a pattern has revealed itself, and it has been the pattern of a cross. And once this pattern has been seen, a strange peace has descended upon the soul: if the mark of the cross is there, all must be well. For as we look into the mists of the past, one dim shape at least can be discerned. It is the shape of a cross. And somehow we know that that cross was the gateway to richer and fuller life. If, then, in existence as we know it, a cross is still to be seen — *sursum corda*. That cross also shall be the prelude to resurrection life.

I

Having then accepted this phrase as apt, in general, to portray human existence, we may go a step farther and claim that there are certain periods of history when it becomes peculiarly applicable to the human situation. Probably at no time is this more the case than in a time of war. There are, indeed, even in times of outward peace, the inward conflicts and struggles which demand consideration and, if possible, interpretation. But in wartime this demand becomes insistent. The conflict is more intense, the contradictions more glaring, the smoke of confusion hangs more darkly over all the scene. Where, then, is the metaphor which can adequately encompass life at such a time? What words can begin to represent the tragedy of human existence as it is then revealed?

It is a remarkable fact that in the midst of the new intensity men seem to turn, without any self-conscious intent, to those images and metaphors which in Christian history have been inseparably connected with the cross. Terms such as redemption, sacrifice, salvation again become current coin. Even the war, which at first sight appears utterly gruesome and horrible, is seen at the second glance to have something of the mark of the cross upon it. Nobility is seen over against brutality, innocent suffering over against stark injustice, self-sacrifice over against callousness. Thus, upon the web of life, even in time of war the cross threads appear, and actually the pattern stands out more vividly than in the quiet days of peace. Men begin to talk in terms of a cross, to think in terms of a cross, to become, if I may use the expression, almost cross-conscious. A few illustrations taken from recent wartime literature will serve, perhaps, to bring home this fact more convincingly to our minds.

II

Consider first how, during these years of war, the word ' sacrifice ' has found its way again into common speech. It is indeed a word which stands for one of the most ancient of all human customs and, from the beginning, has been associated with man's urge to give up some valued possession in order to gain some higher good. Sacrifice then was fundamentally a noble and honourable thing, but in the course of time it came so to be connected with practices that were cruel and degrading that men tended to fight shy of it and even to exclude it altogether from ordinary speech. Yet under the stress of war, when men showed themselves ready and willing to surrender all they held dear in order to safeguard what they deemed to be a still higher good — the safety and freedom of their families and fellow citizens — ' sacrifice ' came into its own again; it seemed the only word that could adequately express the kind of thing they were prepared to do.

not universally true.

I well remember how, at a comparatively early stage of this war, we were deeply moved by the story of the commander of H.M.S. *Jervis Bay*. This ship, which was a merchant cruiser and only lightly armed, was protecting a large convoy of unarmed vessels in their journey across the Atlantic. Suddenly they were attacked by a German pocket battleship, and it seemed that the whole convoy might be exterminated. But without hesitation Captain Fogarty Fegan drew clear of the convoy, set his course towards the enemy, and went into action with all his guns blazing. It was suicide, but it was magnificently successful: through his delaying action, all but four of the merchantmen were saved.

Now the significant thing for our purpose is that the dominant word in the headlines which blazoned abroad the news of the incident was the word ' sacrifice.' Even to the news editors no other word seemed adequate. Probably they had little knowledge of the history and associations of the word, but in a vague way they realized that this was the word of highest dramatic and emotional content to describe the heroic action of the captain and his crew. So it came about that hundreds of thousands of readers were confronted once again with the word ' sacrifice.' Few, if any, stopped to question what it meant. But 'sacrifice' impressed them, moved them, reminded them of half-forgotten things, and came once again into the periphery of their conscious thoughts.

But this is only one example among many. We may glance at another, taken from a responsible monthly and bearing tribute to the heroic struggle of the Polish people. These are the writer's own words:

> " It was Hitler's intention to conquer Russia with Polish help. This was the reason for his pro-Polish policy which lasted into the year 1939. Poland would certainly have lost her independence if she had acquiesced, but she might well have played a big, even if subordinate part, in the conquest and later on in the colonization of Russia. In a purely material sense she would have profited greatly. But she refused. If the war is won it will be the just verdict of history that Poland saved the world and at a fearful price, for of all the countries at war, she has suffered most. If the war lasts a few years longer, it is doubtful whether more than a small minority of the Polish nation will be left alive. . . . Had the Poles shrunk from this sacrifice, Hitler would have had everything. . . . No wonder that his hatred of the Poles is as implacable as his hatred of the Jews." [1]

It would be hard to give higher praise to the people of any nation, but, again, the significant thing for our purpose is that 'sacrifice' is the word which the author feels compelled to use. This giving up of treasured goods in order to make possible a higher good for others — this is the action which men instinctively admire and celebrate. And at no time is it more vividly before their eyes than in time of war. So the word enters again into their vocabulary, and at least *a point of contact is made with the cross, which Christians have always regarded as the perfect example of sacrifice in all human history.* The altar of sacrifice is certainly one place where the threads of life may be seen to cross.

III

Let us consider another group of words which have returned to the common vocabulary during the years of war — the group of words associated with the general idea of ' salvation.' We may cite deliverance, redemption, liberation, and victory: all are concerned with the thought of saving man from the hands of oppressors and tyrants who may have enslaved him. For it is one of the oldest lessons of human experience that there exists in man an insatiable desire to gain control of his fellow, to wield power over some individual or group with whom he is in contact. Up to a point such exercise of power may not be harmful, but when it passes beyond a certain limit, it is bound to involve suffering and misery. So comes the yearning for emancipation and the cry for a leader to liberate and save. But all history shows that salvation is no easy process:

> " It is by no breath,
> Turn of eye, wave of hand, that salvation joins issue
>   with death! "

The tyrant will not readily yield up his prey: only by the payment of a price, the price of hardship and suffering and even death, can the would-be deliverer redeem the enslaved.

Even in days of outward peace man learns that no victory can be gained without cost. In time of war this lesson is brought home with far greater poignancy as the conflict is intensified and the suffering deepened. Salvation and costliness are found to be inextricably bound together: there is no redemption without a ransom. As illustration of the way in which this has been impressed upon our minds in recent days, we need only turn to a volume of Mr. Churchill's speeches delivered during the years 1940 and 1941. By general consent, he has voiced the thoughts of the common people more adequately than any other of the war leaders. What are the words we find him using in relation to the present conflict? He speaks of ' the deliverance of mankind,' of ' decisive victory over the forces of evil,' of ' saving Europe and the world from the curse and tyranny of Nazism,' of ' beating down Satan under our feet,' of ' redemption,' of ' salvation ' which ' will not be denied us.' Over against these terms, however, we find an equally imposing array of striking expressions designed to emphasize the cost which is necessarily involved. He speaks of ' blood and sweat and tears,' of ' pangs and toils,' of ' eternal vigilance,' of ' unrelenting zeal,' or ' grievous cost ' and ' suffering,' of offering freely our very lives that victory may be won. Thus again the cross threads can be seen: salvation and suffering, redemption and ransom, conquest and cost are woven together in the pattern of life and at no time more so than in time of war.

To find one more example of a somewhat different kind, we may turn to another man who has achieved great success in speaking from among the people and for the people. Mr. J. B. Priestley is deeply concerned for the democratic way of life but freely recognizes that much that has gone by the name of democracy has simply been sailing under false colours. In fact, in his judgement, at the outbreak of this war, democracy had almost ceased to exist. Then it was, however, that men of all walks of life rallied to the defence of the freedom they held dear and *by their suffering redeemed democracy*. In saying this, Mr. Priestley is setting forth the view of certain American observers, but it is his choice of language which is significant. The people of Britain, by their suffering, had redeemed democracy and restored a faith for living. Then he continues in words which might be those of a Christian evangelist:

" We must either reject or accept that redemption and faith. There is no mere patting them on the back. Either you deny or you affirm. It is this dilemma that is making some of our more comfortable folks so irritable, so easily angered now. They cannot find it in their hearts to deny and yet they hate to accept and affirm. You can watch their minds squirming and wriggling, trying to find a way out. There is no way out." [2]

This example only serves to reinforce what we have already urged — that under the stress of these days men are using the Christian concepts again, and above all are recognizing in a new way that redemption and salvation can only come through the readiness to suffer and endure.[8] Thus once more *there is a point of contact with the cross, which Christians have always regarded as the supreme act of the divine redemption and the place of the salvation of mankind.* The field of human struggle is another place where the threads of life may be seen to cross.

IV

Still another word which has gained prominence in men's thinking and speaking is the word ' retribution.' It would not be hard to trace the idea that it represents back to the very dawn of man's communal life: it was one of his earliest discoveries that if he were to live in any kind of harmony or peace with his neighbour, both must submit themselves to some higher standard than that of the mere satisfaction of their own immediate whims and desires. If one injured another in any way, he must be prepared to make retribution according to some agreed rule, and in so doing to restore the balance which had been temporarily disturbed. Fundamentally, then, retribution was a just and honourable requirement; it was only as it began to be associated with a vengeful or unforgiving spirit that men came to regard it as undesirable and even degrading. Once again, however, under the sudden stress of war, they were forced to reconsider the whole question afresh. In what sense could the war itself be regarded as the retribution which mankind was being forced to pay for neglected duties and broken laws? In what sense could it be regarded as the exaction of retribution by one group of nations from another group who had transgressed all the decencies of civilized life?

Possibly this concern with retribution has not entered so deeply into the popular mind and vocabulary as has the admiration for sacrifice. And yet there is evidence of a deepening interest in the principles at stake. For instance, important questions have been asked in the British Parliament about the treatment of war criminals, certain of the Law Lords have made pronouncements about the way in which retribution is to be exacted from the Axis powers, and in America Dr. Marcel de Baer, chief of Belgium's judicature, in collaboration with Professor Glueck, of Harvard, has drafted a plan for the punishment of Axis war criminals. Some kind of retribution there must be — of that men are fairly certain; yet how retribution can be exacted without doing injury to the guiltless — of that men are far from certain. Retribution and innocent suffering seem to be inextricably linked together. Some, then, would say that retribution must be demanded without any sentimental regard for the suffering of the relatively innocent; others would say that in view of the bitter suffering which must attend any attempt to enforce justice, the demand for retribution must be finally abandoned. One group cries out for the extermination of every last German and Japanese: nothing less could make retribution for the wrongs they have done. The other group cries out for the cessation of bombing of civilians and for the immediate despatch of food to the starving children of Europe: no retribution that leads to such suffering of the innocent, they hold, can possibly be justified.

Now the significant thing in all this for our purpose is that, without realizing it, men are grappling once again with one of the central problems which have faced all Christian thinkers in relation to the cross. In some way, they feel sure, the cross must stand for the establishment of God's justice; if there is injustice there, then God ceases to count in human affairs. On the other hand, they feel sure that the Victim who suffered there was guiltless and innocent of all wrong: if *he* were guilty, then moral standards have no more place in human life. Such is the dilemma of the cross, and it is the dilemma which is again being brought forcibly home to us by the happenings of war. To speak, as Professor Richard Niebuhr does, of the ' war as crucifixion ' is not just to play with words; it is to give witness to that strange combination of stern justice with innocent suffering which we see both at Calvary and within the war-scarred cities of Europe today.

Thus it is clear that the ideas of retribution and the establishment of justice have again been brought vividly to men's attention. They are never altogether absent from the life of society, but in time of war they are bound to take on a new prominence, for one of the chief motives inspiring a community to engage in so grim an ordeal as armed conflict is the conviction that it is necessary for the re-establishment of justice and the upholding of the right. In this conviction *there is at least a point of contact with the cross, which Christians have regarded as the perfect demonstration of the divine righteousness and the upholding of the moral order of God.* The bar of judgement is another place where the threads of life may be seen to cross.

V

One last word may be mentioned as having taken on an altogether new significance since the beginning of 1940 — it is the word ' regeneration.' What was once associated vaguely in people's minds with sudden conversion, or with controversies about infant baptism, has become vibrant with meaning because of the dramatic events taking place in the world around us. Man has, of course, always been interested in the processes of birth and creation; he has experienced perhaps his moments of sublimest exaltation when new life and new beauty have appeared before his eyes. At the same time, he has dimly realized that even these periods of ecstasy could not be separated from travail and pain. In some strange way death was the pathway to life, travail to joy, suffering to creation. And what had been dimly perceived in days of peace suddenly became an intense conviction in time of war: that somehow suffering and death were not the end, but could lead to creative transformation and the regeneration of life.

Let us first consider an illustration from a war book which has attained a very wide circulation. There is something extraordinarily appealing about the frank revelation of his inmost thoughts which Richard Hillary gives in his book *Falling Through Space*. His heroism and endurance, it need hardly be said, are beyond praise. But what is so significant for our purpose is to notice the way in which a change came over his whole outlook on life as he stood face to face with suffering and death — not so much perhaps his own as that of the friends he loved. His conversations with his great friend Peter's widow are exceedingly moving, and some of her words may be quoted to indicate the effect which suffering has had upon the sensitive mind. " Ever since Peter's death you have been different," she says. " It has worked on you; and it's only because it has, that I tell you these things. Colin says he would never have believed that any one could change as you have. . . . You have given to me in a way that would have been impossible for you before Peter's death. You are still giving. You are conferring value on life by feeling Peter's death as deeply as you do. And you are bound to feel the death, *be re-created by the death* of the others in the squadron — if not in the same degree, certainly in the same way." [4]

A second illustration may be taken from the numerous commentaries which have been written on the event which has shaken our modern world more perhaps than any other — the fall of France. It is remarkable how often the note of regeneration through suffering recurs. For instance, in M. Elie Bois's book *Truth on the Tragedy of France*, he endeavours to show that it was this theory, passively accepted, which was the final cause of her capitulation. He is careful to point out, however, that it was in reality an utter perversion of the truth that was used by Pétain and his circle. They were obsessed by the thought of regeneration coming through suffering and defeat and were prepared, therefore, meekly to surrender. Actually, of course, they were in this way avoiding suffering and agony and were attempting to gain their renewal of life simply by doing nothing. As another writer, M. Alexander Werth, has said: " The old slogan of the Jacobins, ' *Liberté ou la mort* ' had been abandoned for ' *Esclavage . . . plutôt que la mort* ' on the ground that what was most important to save, if anything could yet be saved, was the seeds of national, or rather racial survival. In all this there was a vague conception of ' regeneration through suffering,' and there was the strangely Chinese-like belief that ' France could not be destroyed.' " [5]

In the minds of many of France's leaders, then, the dominating thought was that of evading suffering as far as possible, even at the risk of humiliation and disgrace; they naïvely hoped that out of abject surrender there would somehow spring to life a regenerated people. Far different, of course, has the actual outcome been. Through the capitulation of the leaders, millions of the common people of France have been delivered up to slavery and suffering and death. But for those who now have eyes to see, it is out of *their* agony that the regeneration of the soul of France is to come.

There is a beautiful expression of this essential faith in a book by M. Nattages, who escaped from France and ultimately arrived in England. During the course of his wanderings he crossed the desert, where he noticed what seemed to be an unaccountable green carpet. The driver of his lorry, however, was able to supply an explanation: seeds deposited in the desert by the wind will spring to life years afterwards when blessed by a fertilizing storm. In this phenomenon M. Nattages sees a parable of the regeneration of France.

> " France, whom the world loves, is such a flower, and will be for ever reborn. She has sowed so abundantly, has given so generously to every one. Above all, she has done so much to make the civilized world acquainted with liberty that it will be impossible for the seed she has scattered to be dried up for all eternity by the destructive wind that blows from the east. . . . A beneficent shower will come, gifted by the love and gratitude of a score or more of free peoples, and will make germinate and regerminate, time without end, a flower which has perhaps been over-confident, a trifle heedless, and yet is so beautiful — the flower of liberty which is France." [6]

Thus regeneration and re-creation through travail and agony is, it appears, a lesson which is again being brought home forcibly to the conscience of mankind. Once more, then, *there is a metaphorical relationship to the cross, which all through Christian history has been regarded as the* fons et origo *of all that is divinely fresh and re-creative in human life.* The birthplace of a new creation is another point where the threads of life may be seen to cross.

VI

We have said enough to show that through the stress of war old ideas have again laid hold of men's minds and old metaphors become luminous. Words that had been consigned to the junk heap of theological speculation have been salvaged as valuable wartime material. Men of this generation are realizing as never before that the pattern of life is a cross: words and symbols associated with Calvary have taken on new meaning and returned to everyday use. What, we may ask, is the significance of all this for the life and witness of the Christian Church?

Surely we are justified in inferring that the time is ripe for a new attempt to interpret to our own day and generation what the central cross of all the ages means to human existence. So often in the past this has seemed well-nigh impossible because of the lack of categories, symbols, or parallels from the common life of man which were really familiar and available for immediate use. Men were little concerned about the kind of situation with which the cross was concerned. To speak of redemption or regeneration was to speak into a vacuum. From what we have sought to present in this chapter, it is at least clear that the situation is changing. Can we not, then, turn back again to the cross and try to see how we may recapture its meaning both for ourselves and for those who are showing this new concern about the deepest problems of life?

2. The Cross in the New Testament —
Redemption and Salvation

"And they sung a new song, saying, Thou art worthy to take the book, and to open the seals thereof: for thou wast slain, and hast redeemed us to God by thy blood out of every kindred, and tongue, and people, and nation; and hast made us unto our God kings and priests: and we shall reign on the earth."
— *Rev. 5:9, 10.*

No sane historian would today dispute the fact that Jesus, a prophet of Galilee, was crucified by the order of the Roman authorities at some time within the first half of the first century of our era. Attempts have been made from time to time to categorize this claim of the Christian Church as myth, but such attempts would hardly now be taken seriously. At the heart of the earliest formulated creed of Christendom stands the confession that he, Jesus Christ, was crucified under Pontius Pilate, and thereby Christianity is tied to a particular historical event. Even if the Christian way of life were to be destroyed from off the face of the earth, the fact that Jesus Christ was crucified within human history could hardly be expunged from the annals of the human race.

There is something heartening in this inescapable ' factualness ' of the cross, and yet one is bound to admit that the fact itself, in bare isolation, can have little value for mankind. An event within history, whose meaning no one is able to discern, may affect the purely exterior circumstances of man's life in some small measure; but if it is to play any major part in the development of his inmost soul, then it is essential for

17

it to be viewed as in some sense *meaningful*. This is not to say that the contemporaries of the event, or even their descendants, will necessarily be able to gauge its full significance; in fact, the full meaning may never be grasped by men. At the same time, the extent of its influence will be in direct proportion to the richness of meaning which it is seen to have for the life of the world. Thus in the case of the historical fact of the death of Christ, the event in itself would probably have had little effect upon human history; what has made it, and continues to make it, of immeasurable importance is the meaning that it holds for the inner life of the individual and of society at large.

I

How, then, is this meaning to be first discerned and then disclosed? No question has been of greater importance in the history of the Christian Church, and certainly no question calls for more serious consideration today. At the outset the writer would emphasize that no true answer can be given save in the context of the Holy Spirit. This was the conviction of the early apostles — that it was the Spirit who was taking the events of the life and death of the historic Jesus and revealing their meaning to them. And this same Spirit is ever operating to bring home that meaning in new power to successive generations of Christian disciples. Apart from the inspiration and illumination of the Spirit of Christ, the meaning of his death cannot possibly be discerned.

It is clear, however, that even in New Testament times the conviction that the Spirit was assisting and guiding did not lead the early Christians to abandon all attempts to use meaningful language when they spoke of the death of Christ. Actually we find them using time-honoured words and metaphors which were the best fitted to call up vivid images in their hearers' minds. Such words as ransom, reconciliation, propitiation, and remission may not mean much to present-day readers, but they were certainly vibrant with meaning for those who lived in the first century, and these were the words in common use when reference was made to the Messiah's death. In witnessing to Jews, of course, their task was relatively simple, for the historical tradition of the Hebrews provided a number of words exactly suited to their needs. Amongst the Gentiles, more difficult problems emerged, and there began to be that necessity for fresh interpretation such as has confronted the Church in every new environment and in every new age since that time. In general, however, New Testament writers confined themselves to terms occurring in the Septuagint Version of the Old Testament, and these naturally became significant to converts as soon as they grew at all familiar with the ancient Scriptures.

Thus in the Christian writings of the first century no attempt is made to discuss at length the reasons for the death of Jesus, either from the divine or from the human side. There is no carefully constructed argument, starting from certain premises and advancing towards definite conclusions, with a view to demonstrating the logical necessity of the cross. Rather, we find a number of dramatic accounts of the actual sequence of events and a number of vivid metaphors which serve to describe the significance which these events possessed for Jesus himself and for those who came after. We find also certain names applied to Him who was the central actor in the great drama. If we come to the New Testament expecting to find a cut-and-dried theory of the rationale of the Atonement, we shall be disappointed; if, on the other hand, we come prepared to examine its metaphors and names carefully, and to allow them to quicken our imaginations and enlighten our minds, we shall discover that very thing which the New Testament waits to give to enquiring souls.

C

II

We have just spoken of ' names ' and ' metaphors ' as being specially significant within the New Testament interpretation of the meaning of the death of Christ. A moment's reflection will show why this is so. One of the earliest impulses in human life, if not the earliest, is to attach a name to a person (or thing) to whom one is closely related. A child will attempt to express its reaction to an object which has caught its attention by a name, and one who has grown to adult life is still conscious of the desire to ' name ' a person or thing by placing it within a certain category. Now under normal circumstances persons are named in accordance with the actions they perform or the functions they fulfil. Hence in attempting to assess the significance of a person and the work he has done, it is of the highest importance to pay close attention to the names applied to him by his contemporaries and to the verbs used to describe his actions. In the case of Jesus, then, names and verbal metaphors associated with his person are the most accurate instruments we possess for determining the meaning which his work assumed first for himself and then for those in closest relationship with him.

For it can hardly be seriously suggested that Jesus' life was devoid of all aim or purpose — just borne along on the tide of circumstance with no goal in sight. To read the Gospels is surely to be impressed with the fact that, at least from the beginning of his public ministry, Jesus had a definite conception in mind of what his task was to be. This task may have taken on new aspects and new ranges of relevance as he proceeded, but there was surely an initial vision of what he was intending to do. Now it is questionable whether any man can set out to do something *wholly* new. There are bound to be links of continuity with the past even though, in the course of the outworking of his purpose, new and creative developments may appear. So in the case of Jesus there was no attempt to cut himself off altogether from the past. There was sufficient similarity between what he was intending to do and certain concepts which had emerged in the course of his nation's history for him to be able to employ them in a general way. A particular word-metaphor which men had used to describe a certain action — which they had then applied in ever wider ways, even to the extent of applying it within the realm of man's spiritual relationships — such a word-metaphor Jesus himself could employ in relation to his own future mission. In the same way, the name used in history to describe a person performing such an action could be taken over and used to designate his own particular place within the world of men. The word-metaphor and the name were in no sense final, for what he was to do was in a very real way unique, and the full significance of the words could appear only as his work progressed. Moreover, it was highly desirable that the words chosen should not be too clear-cut in their denotation, lest no room should be left for creative development. Jesus himself would first fill them up with meaning in his own way; then it would be left for the apostolic witnesses to attempt to describe in verbal metaphors the significance of the action which he had performed and to gather all together in certain names which would express what they believed to be the final significance of the One who had acted in their midst as he had done. In seeking to approach the heart of the New Testament interpretation, therefore, we focus attention upon:

1. The verbal metaphors used by Jesus to describe his work.
2. The names which he applied to himself.
3. The verbal metaphors used by the apostles to describe his work.
4. The names which they applied to him.

In this way we believe that we can come nearer to the primal significance of the cross than by any other method.

III

We shall not have gone far in a study of the Gospels before we encounter one metaphor which evidently occupied a leading place in Jesus' thought as he went forth to his ministry: his task was to set his people free. Word-metaphors such as loose, save, deliver, redeem are prominent in the records, and it is these that we must examine with some care. One of the basic experiences of man as such is connected with emancipation from an environment which has become cramping and restricting; he longs to have access to a wider sphere of expansion and freedom. And Jesus saw men bound by disease, by demons, by hard laws, by evil habits, and he was determined to break their bonds and lead them out into freedom and salvation.

But behind all these metaphors, to which we shall refer in more detail below, there stands one event in the history of Israel which in the mind of the average Jew occupied a place of supreme importance. In fact, as Paul Tillich has suggested, this was in reality the centre of all history so far as the Jewish outlook was concerned.[1] This event was the deliverance of the Children of Israel from the bondage of Egypt and their final salvation from the hands of their enemies at the waters of the Red Sea. God had indeed redeemed and saved his people. Thus it is written in Ex. 6:6, 7:

"I will bring you out from under the burdens of the Egyptians, and I will rid you out of their bondage, and I will redeem you with a stretched out arm, and with great judgments: and I will take you to me for a people, and I will be to you a God: and ye shall know that I am the Lord your God, which bringeth you out from under the burdens of the Egyptians."

At once we may notice that there are two sides to that which is here described. From one side the emphasis is on cutting men loose from the bonds of their taskmasters, delivering them from the weight of the oppressive burdens laid upon them by their tormentors; from the other side the emphasis is on the new life of liberty, the expansiveness, the new environment, which has no limits save those of the outreach of God himself. And both of these aspects are envisaged in later references to deliverance in the Old Testament. In Ps. 25, for example, one side is vividly represented. A man pictures himself as in a net: he is enmeshed in troubles and distresses, in afflictions and sins; his enemies surround him on every side. His cry is that he may be ' brought out ' (v. 17) , ' delivered ' (v. 20) , ' set free ' (v. 18) , ' redeemed ' (v. 22) ; he longs to be loosed from all those bonds which hold him in thrall. In Ps. 103, both sides find expression. A man gives praise to God, on the one hand, for loosing him from his iniquities, saving him out of his diseases, and redeeming his life from destruction; on the other hand, for crowning him with loving-kindness and tender mercies and bringing him out into the enjoyment of an expansiveness comparable only to that of an eagle in the heavens. To be loosed from bondage, to enter into liberty — such was the desire and the hope of the true Israelite.

For although there had been the great deliverance at the Red Sea, and although later a certain number had been released from the captivity of Babylon and restored to their own land, the centuries immediately preceding the coming of Christ found a people still looking for God to visit and redeem his people. Some believed that deliverance could only come through armed rising — that God would miraculously support and give victory to those who would challenge the oppressive powers; others believed that man's rôle could only be passive, waiting for God to act in his own good time. But many there were who longed for the ' consolation ' of Israel.[2] It was into this environment that Jesus came. It is significant that in his first recorded public reference to the nature of his mission, the thought of deliverance is predominant. God had anointed him, he said, " to proclaim release to captives, to give sight to the blind, and to set at liberty those that were bruised " (Luke 4:18) . The record of his life shows how the task was accomplished. He loosed the diseased from their infirmities. Rebuking the synagogue ruler who questioned his right to heal on the Sabbath, he said, " Ought not this woman, being a daughter of Abraham, whom Satan hath bound, lo, these eighteen years, to have been loosed from this bond on the sabbath day? " (Luke 13:16) . He delivered the demon-possessed from their slavery. Answering the challenge of those who claimed that he was casting out devils by Beelzebub, he said, " When a strong man armed keepeth his palace, his goods are in peace: but when a stronger than he shall come upon him, and overcome him, he taketh from him all his armour wherein he trusted, and divideth his spoils " (Luke 11:21, 22) . He relieved the heavy-laden of their burdens. In contrast to the religious leaders of his day who by legal precepts bound heavy burdens upon men's shoulders, grievous to be borne (Matt. 23:4) , Jesus proclaimed to all those who were weary and heavy-laden that by coming to him they would find rest to their souls.

Not only, however, did Jesus deliver men from their bondage; he led them out into newness of life. Health for the sick in body (Mark 1:34) , sanity for the sick in mind (Mark 5:15) , self-respect for the despised and outcast (Mark 12:17) , freedom for those bound by ordinances (Matt. 17:26) , such were the benefits which Jesus bestowed upon men. All are included within the one comprehensive term ' salvation,' a word which is specially connected with the *life* of Christ,[3] and which refers in part to present experience while pointing forward also to final blessedness. Deliverance and salvation are two great blessings which came to men through the ministry of Jesus.

But although he " went about doing good, and healing all that were oppressed of the devil " (Acts 10:38), he was clearly conscious of the fact that there was a supreme conflict yet to be fought. He had wrestled with the different powers by which men were enslaved, he had bestowed the gift of new life upon those who had been set free. But something greater and more far-reaching was yet to take place. On the Mount of Transfiguration, he talked with his heavenly visitants concerning the ' exodus ' which he was to accomplish at Jerusalem. Some event comparable to the exodus from Egypt was looming up before him. To his most intimate disciples he spoke mysterious words about a baptism of suffering which he must soon undergo and which he invited them to share. But most striking of all were the words used in describing the ultimate mission of the Son of Man — " not to be served, but to serve, and to give his life a ransom for many " (Mark 10:45). This word ' ransom ' embodies a metaphor so vivid that it deserves a somewhat fuller examination.

Perhaps the most authoritative discussion of the term is to be found in Dr. H. Wheeler Robinson's book *Redemption and Revelation*. He points out that ransom and redemption come from the same root, and that each refers to the process of gaining freedom for a slave by paying an adequate sum for his release. No emphasis, however, is laid on the money payment; all that really matters is the release from the " bond or taboo "[4] which hitherto has bound the oppressed. So in the Septuagint Version of the Old Testament, the verb ' to ransom ' is used of deliverance from sin and death and especially of the deliverance of Israel from Egypt and the exiles from

Babylon.⁵ The great interest of Mark 10:45, then, lies in its revelation of the mind of Jesus as he looked forward to the redemption by which he was to deliver the new Israel out of the house of bondage. In contrast to the two ways by which, in current thought, it was imagined that deliverance might come, Jesus himself set forth the third way: *it would be through the surrender of his own life as a ransom-price to loose men from all the fetters by which they were bound and to lead them out into the glorious liberty of the sons of God.* Thus the final conflict to which he looked forward would, he knew well, demand the expenditure of his very lifeblood; at the same time it would issue i victory and the salvation of the new redeemed people of God. Above all, it would deal finally with the tyranny of sin and would be " at once the repudiation of the service of sin even unto death, and through the ' Red Sea ' of that death the opening of a new way to God." ⁶

IV

We next turn to the question of the name Jesus applied to himself as he conceived his work in this way. We might have expected him to choose such a title as Redeemer (used of Moses in Acts 7:35) or Saviour (used by the Samaritans in John 4:42) or Deliverer. As a matter of fact, however, none of these titles are used by Jesus in the records we have; we must look for a more elusive title to suggest the particular view of his work that we have been considering.

The title which, we believe, Jesus used of himself and which vividly expresses the idea of deliverance and salvation is that of ' Shepherd.' No figure is accorded a higher place of honour in the Old Testament than is the shepherd, and no simile is more often employed in reference to the exodus of the Children of Israel from Egypt than that of a shepherd leading

forth his flock. " He led forth his own people like sheep, and
guided them in the wilderness like a flock. And he led them
safely, so that they feared not " (Ps. 78:52, 53). " Thou leddest
thy people like a flock by the hand of Moses and Aaron " (Ps.
77:20). Looking forward then to the new redemption, the
prophets were constantly employing the shepherd-imagery.
At present, they held, Israel was under the control of false
shepherds who were leading them to ruin (Ezek., ch. 34).
But in days to come the flock would be rescued from bondage,
gathered together and led across the wilderness to its true
pasture. In words of rare beauty, the Second Isaiah describes
the lambs being gathered in the arm and carried in the bosom
(Isa. 40:11), and Jeremiah depicts the flock being gathered
in from their slavery in far countries, home to their rightful
fold (Jer. 23:3; 31:10). Sometimes the work of deliverance
is regarded as performed by God himself, but more often the
Messiah is spoken of as the Shepherd. (Cf. Micah 5:4; Ezek.
34:23; Ps. of Sol. 17:40 *seq.*) Commenting on the oracle in
Ezekiel, Dr. Ryder Smith says:

> " Under the concept ' shepherd,' the idea of force is in
> the background and the idea of salvation in the fore-
> ground, for it is the one duty of a shepherd to ' save '
> his sheep from every kind of harm. It is made a charge
> against the false shepherds that ' with force and with
> rigour have they ruled over ' the flock, whereas they
> ought to have ' sought that which was lost,' and so on.
> The idea runs through the oracle that a true shepherd is
> strong, patient and pitiful. No shepherd here ' gives his
> life for the sheep,' but the true shepherd — whether
> Jehovah or David — will spend his strength for the sheep
> and so ' save ' them." [7]

When we turn to the New Testament " this rich and impressive metaphorical language comes to rest with its application to Jesus as the true Shepherd of the people of God." [8]
It cannot be by chance that Jesus so often refers to his relation

with the people or his disciples as that of a shepherd with his sheep (Mark 6:34; Luke 12:32; 15:3–7; Matt. 15:24). Even during his earthly ministry he acted as shepherd, seeking and saving that which was lost. And he looked forward to the day when he would bring in the other sheep, so that at length there might be one flock and one Shepherd (John 10:16). Before that could come to pass, however, a great deliverance must take place. It was his purpose to be the second Moses, the Shepherd who would lead God's flock out from the bondage of their present state into the freedom of the flock of God. But this would not be without cost. In Mark 14:27 a quotation is taken by Jesus from the prophecy of Zechariah and made to apply to himself. He was to be the Shepherd who would be smitten, and for the moment the sheep would be scattered; but, as he immediately goes on to say, he would be raised up again and would then lead his flock along the way of God's choice. Similarly in the great passage of John, ch. 10, the ' whole parabolic heritage,' to use Hoskyns' term, comes to its focus in the picture of the shepherd who lays down his life for the sheep. " I am the good shepherd," said Jesus. " I lay down my life, that I might take it again. I am come that they might have life, and that they might have it more abundantly." As Canon Phythian-Adams vividly expresses it, " Through His Death and Passion, Christus Pastor is essentially Christus Victor." [9] Thus by designating himself the Shepherd, Jesus was able to set forth his work as the deliverance of God's people from bondage, and the gift to them of abundance of life.

Yet, while regarding himself as the Shepherd of God's flock, may he not also have regarded himself as the Lamb? On the night of Israel's redemption, it was the Passover lamb whose life had been yielded up, to provide the ransom for the first-born, and in Isa., ch. 53, we read that the Servant " is brought as a lamb to the slaughter, and as a sheep before her shearers is dumb." Knowing, as we do, how prominent a place these Scriptures held in the mind of the Lord, is it fanciful to think that he conceived the laying down of his life as comparable to that of the Lamb whose life was given in order that the people might go free? [10] He too would redeem the many by submitting himself to suffering and death. But that would not be the end: he would, by his resurrection, lead forth the many into newness of life. Shepherd — Lamb: this is one of the supreme paradoxes of Jesus' ministry. Redeemer — Ransom: it is the same paradox under another form. In this way only could the flock be delivered out of bondage into their true home within the fold of God.

V

Having sought to view the cross, as it were, from one side, we come now to the witness of the early apostles as they viewed it from the other side. In the early chapters of The Acts, we cannot escape from the dominant feeling of exultation which filled the hearts of the disciples. For the moment, it seems, they were not so concerned with what the death of Christ had effected but rather with the new life which had been made available through his resurrection. The great word is ' salvation.' " Neither is there salvation in any other: for there is none other name under heaven given among men, whereby we must be saved " (Acts 4:12) . " To us is this word of salvation sent " (Acts 13:26). Through the resurrection and exaltation of Christ new life and new power had become available for mankind.

It is when we come to the writings of Paul, however, that the twin notes of redemption and salvation which we stressed earlier come to fullest expression. Taking first the references to redemption, we find that in The Epistle to the Galatians Paul uses the word to describe his emancipation from the bondage of the Law. He was deeply conscious of the far-reaching implications of the Deuteronomic injunction, "Cursed is every one that continueth not in all the things which are written in the book of the Law to do them" (Deut. 27:26). He knew that he could not attain to this standard of perfection: there was no possibility, then, of his avoiding the bondage of the curse of the Law. He seems almost to regard this curse as a spell which had been laid upon him and from which there was no hope of breaking free. Yet, he triumphantly cries, "God sent forth his Son . . . to deliver them who were in subjection to the law" (Gal. 4:4, 5), and, "Christ redeemed us from the curse of the law, having become a curse for us" (Gal. 3:13). How exactly the deliverance took place is not described in detail, but the apostle's general thought is well represented by C. A. Anderson Scott when he writes:

> "He [Jesus] was identified with His race as it lay under the judgement of a broken Law; and the form of His death proved the completeness of the identification. But . . . His triumph over that death which spelled curse, meant triumph over the Law which imposed the curse and the deliverance of His people from its yoke. . . . He broke the power of the Law as a yoke of bondage by first realizing in His own Person the utmost extremity of its authority, and then by breaking forth from its dominion in the newness of the resurrection life. . . . Christ, therefore, was 'the end of the law . . . to every one that believeth' (Rom. 10:4). He was the end of the Law as a system, a dispensation and a servitude." [11]

What has just been said of the Law, moreover, is equally true of the other tyrants envisaged by Paul. In his dramatic way, he regards sin as a tyrant which holds men in thrall. Yet we have "redemption through his blood, even the loosing from our sins" (Eph. 1:7). Through faith in Christ, externalized in baptism, a man died out from under the dominion of sin; he passed into the new domain of God's grace, living in the freedom of the new life in Christ Jesus (Rom., ch. 6). In like manner, the tyranny of death was broken through the death and resurrection of Christ Jesus. Finally there was the servitude to evil spirits which had been very real to Paul, but from which he believed men had also been delivered by the victory of Christ. This concept is not easy for us to grasp today, but there is no doubt that it held a prominent place in the thought of the Early Church. There were principalities and powers, there were things in heaven and things in earth and things under the earth, all of which had been subjugated by Christ and robbed of their dominion over men. How the death of Christ was related to this deliverance is set forth in an important passage (Col. 2:15) which demands some consideration.

In the writer's judgement, by far the most satisfactory interpretation of this difficult passage has been given by C. A. Anderson Scott in the work to which reference has just been made. Translating the verse, " He stripped off from himself the principalities and the powers and made them a contemptible exhibition when by His Cross He triumphed over them," he goes on to point out that according to Paul's general thought it was the ' flesh ' of man through which both sin and the evil spirit-forces laid hold of him and enslaved him. Not that the ' flesh ' was in itself corrupt: only, from the time of the Fall, it had constituted the avenue through which these powers of evil could approach a man and cajole him and conquer him. Now it was fundamental to Paul's thought that Christ had truly assumed human flesh (Rom. 8:3; Gal. 4:4). But whereas in the case of all others the flesh had provided the field for the activity of evil, in His case sin and the powers of darkness were able to make no impression upon his integrity. Finally, in the supreme act of Calvary, by divesting himself of his flesh-body, he laid aside the last medium by which the hostile powers might have attained control over him. " It was they who ' crucified the Lord of glory ' but in doing so they over-reached themselves. He escaped from their dominion, nay more, He broke it; God raised Him from the dead, and in His resurrection (the thought of which is never far from Paul's mind when he is speaking of the Cross) He asserted and proclaimed His victory over every hostile Force, death, demons and the Devil." [12]

We have dwelt at length on St. Paul's references to deliverance and redemption, for nowhere else in the New Testament are the metaphors developed so impressively. When we consider the other aspect of his thought — the references to the more positive state into which Christ had brought men by his victory — it is hard to make any selection, so numerous are the passages. Salvation is a term which he uses in reference to a definite event in the past, to an ongoing experience in the present, and to a final consummation in the future. Attention has often been called to this fact, but it provides the clearest possible testimony to the place which salvation held in the apostle's thought. Salvation involved a great deliverance in the past, a rich experience in the present, and a confident hope for the future — all made possible through the death and resurrection of Christ. And just as he emphasizes the thought of a positive salvation again and again, so too he repeatedly refers to that freedom wherewith Christ had made men free. Galatians and Romans are both ringing declarations of the freedom available to men through the work of Christ. Being made free from the Law and from sin and become servants to righteousness and to God, men could bring forth fruit unto holiness and in the end enjoy everlasting life. There is no finer phrase in the New Testament than St. Paul's summary description of the positive status of redeemed souls — " the liberty of the glory of the children of God " (Rom. 8:21).

It is unnecessary to examine in detail the further references in the New Testament to the ideas of redemption and salvation. Redemption is to the fore in The First Epistle of Peter with its poignant reference to the deliverance from a life of worthlessness through the costly payment of the very lifeblood of Christ. It is to the fore also in the great hymns of the Apocalypse with their references to Him who loved us and " loosed us from our sins by his blood " (Rev. 1:5) and who purchased unto God with his blood men out of every tribe, and tongue, and people, and nation (Rev. 5:9) . In none of these passages is there the suggestion of a *quid pro quo;* rather, the whole emphasis is on the surpassing costliness of the process by which the Son of God had delivered men from their bondage. On the more positive side it is in The Epistle to the Hebrews that we find the greater stress on the concept of salvation. The author is appalled at the thought of regarding lightly a salvation which is " so great " (Heb. 2:3) ; it is a salvation which is " eternal " (ch. 5:9) ; it is a salvation which covers every aspect of human existence (ch. 7:25) . Salvation, in fact, is wholeness in every department of life.

Thus we have found abundant evidence to show that the metaphors of redemption and salvation were employed from the earliest times by Christian witnesses as they sought to describe what Jesus had done. He had delivered man from every form of bondage by his own willing surrender to death; he had saved man into the enjoyment of the fulness of life by his glorious resurrection. We were redeemed by his blood, we are saved by his life — such is the double emphasis of the New Testament writers who had been led out from the Egypt of their own bondage into the promised land of freedom and life.

VI

It remains to confirm what we have discovered so far, by

calling attention to the names given to Christ by those who bore witness to his redeeming and saving power. First of all, in connection with the main thought of the deliverance of the Children of Israel from the servitude of Egypt, there is evidence that Jesus was regarded in a real sense as a second Moses. In Acts 3:22, Jesus is definitely compared to the prophet like unto Moses whom God would raise up for his people, and Stephen later makes the same comparison. More noteworthy, however, are the references to Jesus as the Shepherd of God's flock. Possibly, in certain places, the more pastoral connotations of the title tend now to predominate, but certainly in the reference of Heb. 13:20 to the great Shepherd of the sheep who had been brought again from the dead, there is the reference to the way in which he was designated Leader of God's new Israel, bringing them out of bondage into newness of life. Probably, too, the title of " the Lamb " which we find applied to Jesus in the Fourth Gospel and the Apocalypse carries similar associations. In the Apocalypse they sing the song of Moses and the Lamb, for as Moses had led out the people of old, so the Lamb is now the Leader, and his people follow him whithersoever he goeth (Rev. 14:4). Through his blood they have overcome the Devil, and have been purchased to God out of the earth. The horned lamb was apparently a well-established symbol for the Leader of God's flock in the apocalyptic literature, and it was natural, therefore, to apply it to Him who had redeemed to himself a people for his own possession.[18]

The most important titles, however, are two which are coupled together in Acts 5:31 and which exactly correspond to the two aspects of Christ's work which we have considered in this chapter. " The God of our fathers raised up Jesus, whom ye slew and hanged on a tree. Him hath God exalted with his right hand to be a *Prince* and a *Saviour*." The first of these titles (Greek, *archēgos*) occurs only four times in the

New Testament, twice in The Acts (3:15; 5:31) and twice in
The Epistle to the Hebrews (2:10; 12:2). It has been pointed
out that it was sometimes used in reference to the cult-god
of certain pagan communities, but its use here is almost certainly to be derived from parallels in the Septuagint. In the
moment of dismay after the return of the spies, the Children
of Israel cry out for an *archēgos* who will lead them back to
Egypt; in The Book of Judges, the people persuade Jephthah
to be their *archēgos* in order that he may lead them out to
battle against their foes. Thus the translation of Heb. 2:10
is probably as appropriate as could be found. Jesus is the *Captain* of salvation who leads his people out from bondage and
acts as their champion in the struggle with their foes.[14]

The second title is much more common, both in the Bible
and also in the general usage of the Graeco-Roman world. It
was, for instance, often employed in reference to distinguished
Roman emperors — Claudius, Vespasian, Trajan; there are
inscriptions according them the honour of being saviour of
the world or saviour of all men. Again, however, it is to the
Old Testament that we must look for the normative use of
the term. When Syria oppressed Israel, " the Lord gave Israel
a saviour, so that they went out from under the hand of the
Syrians " (II Kings 13:5) ; when other powers had dominion
over them and the Children of Israel cried unto the Lord,
" the Lord raised them up a saviour " (Judg. 3:9, 15) . In the
Second Isaiah, the title is adopted several times by God himself to describe his relationship to his people: he is the just
God and the Saviour who will deliver his people out of their
evil estate. It was natural, then, that this title should have been
taken over by the Early Church and applied to our Lord,
though there are actually fewer occurrences of it than we
might have expected. It is to be found in St. Paul's great
evangelistic address in Acts, ch. 13, and it may well be that it
was more commonly employed in the Gospel-preaching of the

Church than in the teaching of which the New Testament mainly consists. The later writings do indeed use it more frequently, and the climax is perhaps reached in John 4:42 and I John 4:14, where Jesus is referred to as the Saviour of the world. He, rather than the emperor, is worthy of this high dignity, than which no higher could be found.

We have said enough to show that as the Early Church sought to name the One who was the object of their devotion, they turned to titles indicative of redemption and salvation. Prince and Saviour, Captain and Life-Bringer: such titles he was worthy to bear, who had brought them out of darkness and oppression into the new land of liberty and light and eternal life.

3. The Cross in the New Testament —
Judgement and Justification

"Jesus our Lord . . . who was delivered for our of-fences, and was raised again for our justification."

— Rom. 4:24, 25.

I

At the conclusion of the song of Moses and the Children of Israel recorded in Ex., ch. 15, there is a remarkable verse. Exultantly the singers have proclaimed the mighty saving acts of God: " He hath triumphed gloriously. . . . Pharaoh's chariots and his host hath he cast into the sea." " Thou in thy mercy hast led forth the people which thou hast redeemed: thou hast guided them in thy strength unto thy holy habitation." Then they look into the future: "Thou shalt bring them in, and plant them in the mountain of thine inheritance." Finally comes the grand climax: " The Lord shall reign for ever and ever." Thus the thought which immediately follows the experience of redemption and salvation is that of the kingship of Yahweh; it is to this thought that we shall now direct our attention.

When exactly the idea of the kingship of Yahweh came to be accepted in Israel we cannot say, though certainly from the time of the receiving of the Law at Sinai, Yahweh was conceived as Lawgiver and Judge. For a while, no attempt was made to express this authority through the medium of an earthly kingship, but ultimately Israel followed the example of other nations and appointed one of its number, Saul, to exercise sovereign rights within the community. Later records portray Saul as a weak and unfaithful monarch, but he was succeeded by the one who came to be regarded as the man after God's own heart. Under his rule Israel and Judah were

37

united, a succession of victories over foreign powers were won and peace and order were established in the land. As the writer of The Second Book of Samuel expresses it: " David reigned over all Israel; and David executed justice and right-eousness unto all his people " (ch. 8:15). In fact, the period of his rule stood out in the memory of the nation as the time when the kingship of Yahweh was realized in a quite unique way. In consequence, there was a general tendency to look forward with longing expectation to the appearance of a sec-ond David, who would once again make the kingship of Yah-weh a reality on the earth.

This does not mean, of course, that there was any marked decline in the sense that Yahweh himself was King over all. In the writings of the prophets and in The Psalms may be found constant references to the fact that Yahweh is King. " Thy kingdom is an everlasting kingdom, and thy dominion endureth throughout all generations " (Ps. 145:13). At the same time, there was ever the hope that in some way or other that Rule would once again be established upon the earth, and this hope gradually crystallized itself into various forms.

On one matter, indeed, almost all were agreed — it would be a *righteous* kingdom. " Behold, a king shall reign in right-eousness " — that was the utterly important matter so far as the prophets were concerned. And it was a view shared in large measure by all schools of Hebrew thought. " The idea that God will in the end establish righteousness, prosperity and peace among men is all but universal in Hebrew thought. It is found alike in Deuteronomic and Prophetic writings. Again, the idea is frequent in the psalms. Even the psalms of the suffering poor presuppose that the God with whom they plead is able to help, and that, since he is righteous, he will in the end surely help. Again, the apocalyptic idea would be meaningless unless the apocalyptists counted on the ultimate reign of righteousness. They all declare that, however terrible the process, at the last God will vindicate himself by making 'a new heaven and a new earth wherein dwelleth righteousness.' " [1] When, however, it came to defining *how* the Kingdom would be established, there was a wide diversity of opinion.

In certain quarters, emphasis tended to be laid upon purely national sovereignty to be attained by military conquest. From time to time there would be fierce outbreaks of this spirit but they were often short-lived and on the whole it is doubtful whether this conception of the Kingdom had any widespread influence. More important were two general schools of thought, one of which laid the whole emphasis upon the necessity for ethical purity and religious devotion in order that the Kingdom might be established, and the other of which set all its confidence upon a divine intervention which should usher in the Kingdom in great power. The first outlook led, ultimately, to an extreme development of legalism: if only two Sabbaths could be perfectly kept, it was said, the Kingdom of God would come. Nevertheless, there was a development of real piety amongst those who accepted ' the yoke of the Kingdom of Heaven,' a phrase which denoted a wholehearted devotion to God and a determination to obey his commands.

Similarly the second outlook tended to foster an extreme kind of fanaticism: there were those who were disposed to force God's hand, as it were, by exhibitions of wild recklessness. Yet there was something splendid about those who lived in the spirit of The Book of Daniel, fasting and praying and waiting upon God to take to himself the power and reign.

How far these ideas extended among different groups of people we have little means of knowing, but at least we can say that there was within Judaism both the hope of the establishment of God's rule on earth and the conviction that this rule would be a righteous rule, involving judgement upon all that was contrary to God's will and the vindication of those who were accepted of him.

II

After the briefest possible introduction, our earliest Gospel brings us face to face with the chief concern of Jesus' ministry. "Now after that John was put in prison, Jesus came into Galilee, preaching the gospel of the kingdom of God, and saying, The time is fulfilled, and the kingdom of God is at hand: repent ye, and believe the gospel." Into the precise meaning of the phrase ' is at hand ' it is not necessary for us to enter. Suffice it to say that there is a growing measure of agreement among scholars that the manifestation of the Kingdom as Jesus conceived it was not simply immediate, nor simply in the future. There seems to be ample evidence to show that in a real sense Jesus regarded the Kingship of God as already present, in and through his own life and work; at the same time there is further evidence which suggests that he regarded the Kingship as about to be established in greater power. Each of these aspects must be considered in more detail.

As far back as we can go in the history of mankind, we find certain systems of taboos which served to guarantee a certain orderliness within human society. Violations of the taboos were believed to receive automatic punishment: immunity from harm simply proved that the person concerned was guiltless. Gradually, however, infringements of the rules of society were dealt with in more deliberate fashion; officials of the society were appointed to execute the judgement which had been decided upon by the supreme authority. Thus the king or the judge or his representative administered judgement; only after this had been carried into effect could a guilty man be restored to his proper place within the society to which he belonged. Thus to inflict a penalty and restore to favour are two of the oldest actions of human history.

Now it may be asked, Are these twin actions to be found anywhere in the ministry of Jesus? We believe that this question must be answered with a decided affirmative. In the first place there are numerous indications of judgement being executed upon demons. This may seem strange to us today but there is no doubt at all that this judgement was regarded as one of the clearest evidences of the Kingship of God being manifest upon earth. In the synagogue incident in the first chapter of Mark, Jesus stands forth in his rôle as Judge, sternly rebukes the demon, orders him out of the man and thereby sends him forth to destruction; and the people were amazed at the authority, the mark of royal judgement, which had appeared in their midst. Similarly in the account of the man named Legion, whatever difficulties there may be in the story, the chief point of it is the judgement which was meted out upon these evil forces. In sending them to their doom in the abyss, Jesus was undoubtedly manifesting the kingly authority of God. The comment of Jesus recorded in both Matthew and Luke gives the strongest possible confirmation of what has just been said: " But if I by the finger [Matthew: ' Spirit '] of God cast out devils, then is the kingdom of God come upon you." In the judgement inflicted upon the demons and, in the restoration to sanity of their victims, the Kingship of God was already being realized among men.

But it is in relation to men that we most clearly see the twofold process of judgement and vindication at work. We shall consider first Jesus' relations with the sick and secondly his relations with the outcast. A particularly vivid example of the former is to be found in the story of the leper in Mark, ch. 1, and we are indebted to Canon Alan Richardson for a most illuminating commentary on the story.[2] He points out that the reading ' being angry ' in verse 41 is probably to be preferred to the easier reading ' moved with compassion.' If this is correct, then immediately we have a burning expression of judgement — upon the sin, of which the leprosy was the symbol. But this is followed at once by Jesus' action in stretching forth his hand and touching the leper, " thereby taking upon himself the burden of defilement. He is revealed by this symbolic action as the sin-bearer." Finally the leper is justified or vindicated as he goes to offer the things which Moses had commanded. " The whole Pauline doctrine of justification by faith is expounded in this short pericope, which carries us to the very heart of the Gospel message of forgiveness." Other examples of healing may not be so striking but at least it may be claimed that in every case there was the cancellation of the judgement of the sickness which symbolized the sin and the vindication of the sinner by his restoration to health. The Kingdom was being manifested: but already it was involving a cost [3] for the One through whom its judging-vindicating activity was being shown. It is a profound comment of Matthew's Gospel: " Himself took our infirmities, and bare our sicknesses."

In regard to the outcasts of society, we see a similar process being enacted. Publicans and sinners undoubtedly constituted a degraded section within the community and there is no indication that Jesus adopted towards them merely a pleasant, friendly attitude which was quite indifferent to moral realities. Yet by his very presence amongst them, by his very call and invitation to them, he assumed the responsibility for their indebtedness. The fact of their sinfulness was undoubted; so was the fact of the judgement which had already fallen upon them because of their sin; but Jesus was prepared to bear the full weight of both in his own person and to speak the word of acquittal which would send them forth into newness of life. It was his willingness to share their estate which brought them to repentance; repentance was the outward sign that they knew their judgement had been borne away; and as soon as they turned their faces towards God in

true repentance, salvation came to their house (Luke 19:9).
In fact they became justified and restored to God's favour
(Luke 18:14); the Kingship of God was established in their
lives. But for Jesus himself it was a costly process; nothing led
to a greater measure of slander, misrepresentation and even
downright detestation from his contemporaries than the fact
that " he eateth and drinketh with publicans and sinners "
(Mark 2:16).

We have sought to suggest various ways in which the Kingdom of God was manifested in and through the earthly life
of Jesus. He stood beside men in their judgement; he rejoiced
with them in their vindication. Yet he was in no doubt that
all these were only preliminary manifestations of the Kingdom. There was a greater event still to come in which the
Kingdom would be established in power. But how was this
to be enacted? A careful study of the Gospels leaves us in
no doubt concerning the answer to this question. *Only
through the suffering and death of the Son of Man could the
Kingdom be finally established in power and men reinstated
under the true authority of God.*

Three sayings of Jesus in the Gospel of Mark are of special
importance in this connection. The first is that which occurs
in the account of the descent from the Mount of Transfiguration. After referring to the coming of Elijah, Jesus asks:
" How is it written of the Son of man, that he should suffer
many things and be set at nought? But I say unto you, that
Elijah is come, and they have also done unto him whatso-
ever they listed " (Mark 9:12, 13). There are difficulties in
this passage but the main conclusion to be drawn from it is
well set out by Vincent Taylor. " By reason of its association
with the question concerning Elijah, the saying shows that
Jesus thought of his Messianic suffering in relation to the
coming of the Kingdom. He had faced the problem created
by the expectation of the return of Elijah before the Parousia,

and had solved it by identifying Elijah with John; but he had also faced a problem not contemplated in the thought of the time — the necessity of the suffering of the Son of Man before the perfecting of the Rule of God. This problem he had solved in the certainty of his own suffering and rejection." [4] The other sayings occur on the very eve of his passion and reveal how the thought of the Rule of God was still uppermost in his mind: " I will no more drink of the fruit of the vine, until that day when I drink it new in the kingdom of God " (Mark 14:25). " I appoint unto you a kingdom, even as my Father appointed unto me " (Luke 22:29). The high importance of both these sayings, as Vincent Taylor also points out, is that they show clearly that " the idea of the Kingdom, so central in His Galilean teaching, was His sure hope and confidence in the very shadow of the cross. He did not renounce His earlier teaching and replace it by the idea of a redemptive sacrifice. On the contrary He is still sure that the Kingdom will be established; He will yet drink the wine of the Messianic banquet. The ring of joyful confidence is unmistakable. This hope can only mean that He believed His death to be a necessary step to the establishment of the Kingdom. He must suffer and die, then the Rule of God can be consummated; this, and nothing less is the implication of His words." [5] The *necessity* of the cross for the full establishment of the Kingdom seems to be well attested by these sayings; light on the *way* in which the cross was to work towards that end will, it is hoped, be derived from the next section of our study.

III

One of the most remarkable features of Jesus' ministry is the way in which he seemed deliberately to avoid the name of Messiah. This has become a commonplace in the modern study of the Gospels and need only be mentioned, in order

to explain why there is no need to pay any particular attention to it at this point. It is true that Jesus did not entirely
refuse the title, and the confession of Peter and the challenge
of the high priest taken together make it abundantly clear that
Jesus did regard himself as the Messiah in a certain sense.
His reticence is usually interpreted as an indication that he
could not accept any of the meanings of the title current in
his day, and there seems no reason to question this explanation. He was certainly not a warrior-king; he was certainly
not a supramundane figure suddenly bursting into history
before the astonished gaze of his contemporaries; neither was
he a wonder-worker, concealed for a while in the desert and
later performing miraculous works for the benefit of his people.[6] And these were not the only views of the nature and
character of the looked-for Messiah held at the time. The
actual title, then, he avoided, even though it was perfectly
evident that he had come to perform Messiah's work. Instead
he chose two other titles and combined them in a dramatically impressive way. He was the Son of Man who would fulfil his Messianic mission by acting as the Servant of the Lord.

As is well known, in the Marcan story the term 'Son of
man' appears on Jesus' lips only twice during the period
of his ministry prior to the confession of Peter at Caesarea
Philippi. In consequence it has been argued by Dr. T. W.
Manson that these earlier uses are to be regarded in a different way from the later: that whereas in Mark, ch. 2, the term
simply stands for 'Man in the Kingdom,' the later uses refer
to Jesus in company with his disciples or to Jesus standing
alone. It is questionable, however, whether such a distinction
should be made. If reference is made to Mark, ch. 2, it will
be seen that the title is used in connection with Jesus' claim
to possess authority to remit sins. When questioned by the
Pharisees, he called upon the man to rise up and walk and thus
show openly that the penalty attached to his sin had been re-

moved. For whether or no Jesus accepted the generally recognized connection between disease and sin, certainly to the bystanders and to the man himself healing was the clearest possible proof that the debt or punishment had been cancelled. Moreover, the use of the term ' my son ' was surely also an indication of his restoration to favourable regard. In fact, there could be no more vivid illustration of the essential work of the Son of Man — it was to act as vicegerent for God, remitting sins and justifying the guilty.

Turning to the second use of the term at the end of the chapter, we find it in the context of the Sabbath controversy. On no point of the legal system of his day does Jesus appear to have taken such sharp issue with the Pharisees. To all intents and purposes, the Sabbath had become an absolute in current regard and Jesus challenged such an idolization with all his power. In fact he acted as Judge even over the religious law of his day. " The Son of man is Lord " — yes, over every ordinance of man. The Son of Man alone can justify or condemn — not the Pharisees or any other religious leaders. In this phrase " The Son of man is Lord " there is surely the archetype of one great strand of New Testament Christology.

Thus, as Son of Man, even in the days of his earthly ministry, Jesus was able to move amongst men, judging and acquitting. When, however, we reach the period beginning at Caesarea Philippi, we become conscious of a growing tension in Jesus' mind. As Dr. J. W. Bowman has pointed out in his valuable examination of the meaning of the term ' Son of Man ' on Jesus' lips, from this time forward the term is used in two main connections.[7] In one group of passages the motif of *exaltation* predominates; in the other group, the motif of *humiliation*.

According to the latter group, the Son of Man is to " suffer many things, and be rejected of the elders, and of the chief priests, and scribes, and be killed, and after three days rise again " (Mark 8:31). According to the former group, he will sit on the right hand of power, and come in the clouds of heaven (Mark 14:62); and he will pronounce the final judgement on the nations of the earth (Matt. 25:31). Are we not, then, to infer from this evidence that Jesus looked forward to (a) a crucial experience of judgement and vindication in which he was to be the central figure, and (b) a final judgement and vindication when men would stand before the Son of Man, the Judge of all, the Vindicator of the righteous? If this is so, then we may claim that the second part of this expectation was in many ways in line with the traditional conception of the Son of Man. The first part, however, is so utterly out of line that it can only be explained on the assumption that Jesus was here introducing something entirely new: the new thing, as has so often been shown, was the group of ideas which surrounded the Isaianic Servant of the Lord.

It is not necessary to examine at length all the passages in the Synoptic Gospels where reference is made to the Servant.[8] It is true that Jesus never actually called himself the Servant but the references to the Servant prophecies are so obvious in, e.g., Mark 8:31; 9:31; 10:45; Luke 22:37, that no reasonable doubt can be entertained that Jesus identified himself, in at least a general way, with the figure there delineated. This fact is of the greatest significance. For what is the essential character of the work of the Servant? " He bare the sin of many "; he shall justify many since he bears their iniquities: this double-sided mission of sin-bearing and justifying is without doubt the supreme ' service ' which by his suffering and death the Servant performs.

If now we connect this with what has been said above about the Son of Man, the following significant result is obtained. Taking over the concept of Son of Man, a title which in the later years of Judaism had been applied to the representative of the Most High who would act as Judge and vicegerent amongst men, Jesus applied it to himself when, during his ministry on earth, he exercised the authority of Judge and Vindicator in relation to individuals. Moreover, he used it in looking forward to the future Day of the Lord when he would act as Judge and Vindicator in relation to all mankind. In reference to the immediate future he used it, but only in a distinctly modified sense. There was to come a crisis in which he, the Son of Man, Judge and Vindicator, would himself be judged and vindicated. Acting in the manner of the Servant of Isaiah, he would bear the judgement of many as he submitted himself to suffering and death. But that would not be the end: he would be finally vindicated by the resurrection from among the dead, and in and through his own vindication he would justify the many. Son of Man — Servant of God: this is one of the supreme paradoxes of Jesus' ministry. Judge and Vindicator — judged and vindicated: it is the same paradox in another form. In this way only could ' the many ' be brought to their true place under the sovereign rule of God.

IV

Attention has often been drawn to the fact that whereas in the Synoptic Gospels the Kingdom of God is a concept which takes a larger place in the record than any other, in the later books of the New Testament the references to it are comparatively few. Particularly is this the case in the writings of Paul. Proud as he was of his own Roman citizenship, we might have expected him to present a greater development of the thought of God's Kingdom, but actually this never occurs. Yet, when we look closer, we find that although the phrase ' Kingdom of God ' is only rarely to be found, that aspect of the economy of the Kingdom which we saw was so prominent in the Old Testament comes to the very forefront of his

thought. It is the ' righteousness of God ' which is the leading
term in Paul's Epistles, and this righteousness is closely linked
with the Kingdom. " The kingdom of God," cries the apostle,
" is not meat and drink; but righteousness, and peace, and
joy in the Holy Ghost " (Rom. 14:17). To establish God's
righteousness is, in effect, to establish his Kingdom.

No question loomed larger in the mind of young Saul of
Tarsus than that of how this righteousness was to be attained.
He set himself to keep the Law with unexampled vigour and
enthusiasm until as " touching the righteousness which is in
the law " he was blameless. Yet the more scrupulously he
obeyed the injunctions of the Law, the more his sense of sin
and shortcoming deepened (Rom. 3:20; 7:23, 24) until he
stood convinced that no human efforts could lead either to the
justification of man or to the establishment of the righteousness of God. Then it was that the revelation broke upon his
soul that through the righteous life of Jesus Christ poured out
in death, God had established his own righteousness in the
world and at the same time had reinstated sinful man in his
favourable regard.[9] He had openly demonstrated his righteousness upon the plane of history — in fact in a very real
sense God's Kingdom had already been proleptically established at Calvary; furthermore, he had, in and through the
atoning death of Christ, cancelled man's indebtedness and
justified him already at the bar of the divine judgement. He
who had been justified at the cross would certainly pass scathe-
less through the final assize (Rom. 5:9).

The whole matter is summed up in a striking verse (Rom.
4:25) where Paul asserts that Jesus our Lord was delivered
up for our trespasses and was raised for our justification. Here
we note at once that the first half of the verse is an almost
verbatim quotation from Isa. 53:12, and we find a link with
the insistence of Jesus himself that his death was designed to
fulfil the purpose of the Servant's death, viz., to bear the sin

of many. By the death of Jesus, in other words, man's debt
of sin had been annulled in a way consonant with God's righteousness. The second half of the verse, however, states that by
the rising again of Jesus, man had been justified. Vincent
Taylor, following J. Weiss,[10] questions whether this special
relation of the resurrection to justification should be pressed,
in view of the fact that the death and resurrection stand together as effecting man's forgiveness and justification. Certainly no rigid separation can be made between what are,
after all, two sides of one process. Nevertheless, Paul con-
nects justification with life elsewhere (Rom. 5:18) and it is
fitting, therefore, to regard man's restoration to God's favour
as being effected through the great act whereby Christ
himself was vindicated openly and man was vindicated
in him.

One more passage may be mentioned which seems to make
Paul's thought particularly clear. In Rom. 5:12 *seq.*, he dis-
cusses at some length the judgement which fell upon all mankind as the result of Adam's sin. In Paul's view this judgement was death. It was a universal judgement to which all
men were subject: no one could look forward to any other
doom than death. Yet, in point of fact, Jesus Christ became
obedient unto death and thereby submitted himself to the
judgement imposed on sin. Had that been the end, man's doom
would have been sealed. But just as in the case of the paralytic
in Mark, ch. 2, the rising up was the mark that his indebtedness had been cancelled, so in the resurrection of Jesus Christ
there was the unmistakable witness to the fact that man's debt
had been borne and consumed and that man was reinstated
in newness of life.

" As then through the trespass of one man, all were
sentenced to doom, so through one man's act of righteousness, all received acquittal and new life. For as through
the disobedience of one man, many were set in the way

of sin, so through the obedience of the one, many shall be set in the way of righteousness " (Rom. 5:18, 19) .

And to be set in the way of righteousness is to be reinstated as a subject of the Kingdom of God.

V

Coming finally to the question of the titles applied to our Lord by the Early Church, we may first notice the evidence of the apostolic sermons in Acts, chs. 2 to 5. One great contrast to the Synoptic Gospels is immediately evident. Whereas during Jesus' ministry the name Christ was as far as possible avoided, here the title is freely and openly used, and the apostles exult in their assurance that Jesus was verily the Christ. The resurrection had evidently dispelled their doubts: Jesus, they believed, had been exalted to the Messianic throne, and would one day return to final judgement. Meanwhile, their assurance was joyfully expressed in the famous words of Peter: " God hath made that same Jesus, whom ye have crucified, both Lord and Christ " (Acts 2:36) . The risen Christ is the central figure in the early apostolic testimony.

But not only do these chapters reveal Jesus as Lord. Equally they reveal him as ' Servant.' Commenting on Stephen's reference to ' the Righteous One ' (Acts 7:52) , Dr. Ryder Smith writes:

" It is permissible to think that the speech, if it had not been interrupted, would have ended with the claim that Jesus was the Servant of the Lord. This is the more likely since elsewhere (Acts 3:13–15) Jesus is called alternatively God's ' Servant ' and ' the Holy and Righteous One.' . . . It is important to note that here and elsewhere (Acts 2:36; 4:27–30) Luke introduces the name ' Servant ' for Jesus without explanation, for this

E

implies that it was commonly used for our Lord in the Jerusalem Church. . . . It is clear that for the explanation of the Death of Jesus the first Christians turned to the prophecies of the Servant of the Lord." [11]

Christ the Lord, the Servant of God: these are the two titles most prominent in the Early Church.

If we turn to The First Epistle of Peter, a book which seems to represent the general body of ideas held by the second generation of primitive Christianity,[12] we find a similar emphasis on the Christ who performed his work as the Suffering Servant of God. There are two passages in particular which call for consideration. In the first, I Peter 2:21–24, a vivid picture is drawn of the patient sufferings of Christ and of the consequences which flowed from them for the life of mankind. Nowhere, perhaps, in the New Testament are there more direct echoes of Isa., ch. 53, and there can be no doubt that the sufferings and death of Christ were interpreted by reference to that source. What is of particular interest to us, however, is the way in which the judgement-vindication motif predominates. The Servant himself, it is insisted, was completely innocent; he " did no sin, neither was guile found in his mouth: who, when he was reviled, reviled not again; when he suffered, he threatened not." Yet, in spite of his innocence, he suffered. He might have rebelled but instead " he committed his cause to him who judges righteously." In other words, in his suffering righteous judgement was being exercised, even though to the onlooker no connection could be seen between the innocence of the sufferer and the poignancy of the sufferings. The explanation immediately follows. It was *our* sins that he was bearing, *our* responsibilities that he was taking upon himself. As Dr. James Denney pertinently remarks, " The apostle does not raise the question whether it is possible for one to assume the responsibilities of others in this way; he assumed . . . that the responsibilities of sinful men have been taken on Himself by the sinless Lamb of God. This is not a theorem he is prepared to defend; it is the gospel he has to preach." [13] And we may add that though this fact can never prevent us from trying to understand in our own way the connection between his suffering and our sin, it is quite clear that readers of this epistle found nothing strange or abhorrent in believing that Christ actually took upon himself the burden of their judgement and made it possible for them to be vindicated by God. As the writer goes on to say, the outcome of Christ's action has been that our sins and their consequences may be regarded as cancelled — we are dead so far as they are concerned: but the further outcome has been that we may live to righteousness — may live, in other words, the justified life under the sovereignty of God.

The other passage is to be found in I Peter 3:18 *seq.*: " Christ also died for sins once for all, the righteous one on behalf of the unrighteous, that he might bring us home to God." The connection with Isa., ch. 53, is again obvious; so too is the context of the righteousness of God. There was a critical act of judgement; Christ, the Righteous One, died; in his death, it must have been the guilt of the unrighteous that was being cancelled: their indebtedness was removed. But the other side of the process immediately follows. He, in his risen life, justifies us and brings us home to God. " The word προσάγειν," writes Denney, " has always a touch of formality in it; it is a great occasion when the Son who has assumed our responsibilities for us takes us by the hand to bring us to the Father. . . . For those who commit themselves to Christ . . . it is possible to draw near to God and to live in His peace." [14] Whether this precise metaphor is contained in the word or not, it is certainly the case that in the apostle's view those whose judgement has been borne away now have free access to the favour and fellowship of God.

In the epistle we have just considered, Jesus is most com-

monly referred to simply as Christ. But gradually this came
to be little more than a proper name and the other title of
Acts 2:36 took its place. It is in the name ' Lord ' that we find
the continuance of the Messiah-Son of Man traditions; as
Lord, Jesus was regarded as the one to whom authority had
been delegated for the present rule and government of the
Church, and ultimately for the judgement of all mankind. Yet
the ' Servant ' title was not forgotten within the Christian community. Lord-Servant: this is the paradoxical combination
which continues through the whole of the New Testament
Scriptures. In all probability the earliest Christian creed was
simply the confession, " Jesus is Lord " (cf. Rom. 10:8, 9;
I Cor. 12:3) , this being the necessary preliminary to baptism.
At the same time, the very first article of the apostolic Gospel
summarized by Paul in I Cor., ch. 15, is that Christ died *for
our sins* according to the Scriptures, and the phrase ' for our
sins ' must almost certainly be connected with the Servant of
Isa., ch. 53. It is true that the title ' Lord ' tends to be associated specially with the risen Christ in his present reigning
power: he still acts as Judge within the Church (I Cor. 4:4)
and Head of his people (Eph. 1:22). Nevertheless, the Church
is constantly reminded that it was this same Lord who died
for their sins and rose again for their justification; therefore
let them reckon themselves to be dead indeed to sin but alive
to God through Jesus Christ their Lord. Thus the twin themes
of judgement and justification are never far away: men's eyes
are ever being turned towards Jesus, the Sin-Bearer and the
living Lord.

4. The Cross in the New Testament —
Consecration and Communion

"Jesus said unto them, Verily, verily, I say unto you, Except ye eat the flesh of the Son of man, and drink his blood, ye have no life in you." — John 6:53.

I

At the beginning of the previous chapter, we noticed that the hymn of redemption, sung by Moses and the Children of Israel after the deliverance from the Red Sea, concludes with a remarkable reference to the reign of Yahweh. A study of the Exodus narrative will show that its realization in the life of the Israelite people came with the disclosure of the Law at Sinai and the beginning of the ordering of the life of the community according to its injunctions. In a real sense this was the inauguration of Yahweh's rule within the redeemed community. Further study will lead us to the next main stage in the development of their independent nationhood. In Ex., ch. 24, we are first told that Moses recounted to the people the commandments of the Lord and that the people with one voice promised their obedience. Then there follows a series of strange actions: an altar is builded, pillars are set up, sacrifices are offered, blood is taken and put in basins, half of it is sprinkled on the altar, the book of the covenant is read and the people respond, and finally the other half of the blood is sprinkled on the people themselves. Having performed these actions, Moses solemnly declares, " Behold the blood of the covenant, which the Lord hath made with you concerning all these words " (Ex. 24:8) . What is the purpose of all this ceremonial? Have the actions any meaning? Is symbolism of this kind a necessary part of a nation's life?

Without attempting to answer these questions, we shall simply assume that this ceremonial had a meaning for those

55

participating in it and that we may see in it the beginnings of the development of a truly Hebraic culture. These were not merely utilitarian actions; they did not even relate directly to the moral life of the community; yet they were regarded as necessary to the cohesion and continuance of the communal life and as significant within the context of the relations between the people and their God. As we can readily see, the central concept around which the ceremonial revolved was that of the covenant, while the central actions of the ceremonial itself were the offering of the victims and the manipulation of the blood. We must first, then, seek to gain some idea of the significance of a covenant and then of its connection with the sacrificial rites.

If we seek to pierce back into antiquity in order to discover the origin of the covenant idea, we shall find that it is always associated with one particular phenomenon. This is the setting up of a new community distinct from that which has hitherto existed. Thus there may be in any area a community bound together by the ordinary ties of blood and soil. Some sequence of events takes place which leads ultimately to the establishment of a new community, bound together by new ties whose character depends in large measure on the nature of the events which brought the new group into being. This new community in almost every case constitutes itself on the basis of a covenant. If we enquire further concerning the nature of the events we note that it may be certain changes within the *natural* order that bring people together within new configurations or it may be disturbances within the *social* order that lead to the emergence of the new groupings. Normally, however, the covenant is the foundation upon which the new order is built. In cases where the impulse towards the new is derived from happenings within the *natural* order, the covenant usually expresses itself by means of ceremonial actions or sacred objects taken from the natural world. On the other hand, in cases where the impulse is derived from changes within the social order, the covenant is more likely to express itself by means of actions or objects of a symbolic kind. These have their connection, of course, with the natural world but it is their symbolic import to the social group which is of primary significance.

If now we turn to the Old Testament, we find that the covenant idea is in many ways the central concept of the whole collection of writings. It is not for nothing that the title of the book is the Old Testament (i.e., Covenant) for, as Dr. W. F. Lofthouse has remarked, every section of the Hebrew Canon refers to the Covenant. " The Hebrew word (*berith*) ," he says, " is one of very general application. It is used for any kind of bond, agreement or partnership, intended to be permanent or only temporary; for any sort of association, indeed, into which men can enter voluntarily. The compact between Jacob and Laban was a covenant; so was the alliance between Abimelech and Shechem." [1]

Yet, although the word is of such frequent occurrence, there are certain outstanding examples of covenants made between God and man and both of the types mentioned above are to be found. Representative of the first type is the covenant made by God with Noah. The great deluge having taken place, God makes his covenant with all surviving living creatures, both man and beast. To establish the covenant a *natural* phenomenon is appointed — the bow in the cloud — and the new community is dependent upon its recurrence for the renewal of the bond that has been made. A second example may be seen in the covenant with Abraham as recorded in Gen., ch. 17. The priestly writer concentrates attention on a ceremonial action of a physical kind, by which, in his view, the covenant was brought into being. By the rite of circumcision men were purified physically (and, to a degree, psychically) and so made fit to dwell in fellowship with God. The rite was repeated in the case of every new member incorporated within the community and thereby the covenant bond was renewed.

On the other hand, in the account of the Abrahamic covenant given by the prophetic writer in Gen., ch. 15, a different emphasis is to be found, an emphasis which is representative of the second type already referred to. Here attention is focussed upon a ceremonial action of a markedly symbolic kind. Animals are slain, their bodies are divided and each piece laid one against another. Then, in the twilight, a mysterious presence symbolized by a smoking furnace and a burning lamp passes between the pieces of the victims. Various interpretations of the symbolism have been given but none of these can be regarded as fully satisfactory. The important thing to note, however, is that something in the nature of a sacrifice evidently took place, that the fire symbol held a position of central significance and that a communion was regarded as established by Yahweh's acceptance of Abraham's dramatic performance.

So far, then, we have distinguished two kinds of covenants, the one belonging to the natural order of things and established by ceremonies of a more naturalistic type, the other belonging to the social order and established by ceremonies of a more symbolic type. The former kind is seen in the Genesis narratives which derive from the priestly school of thought, the latter in those derived from the prophetic writings.

Coming now to the covenant story with which we began this chapter, we find that it occurs in a prophetic narrative and is concerned specially with the establishment of the social bond between Yahweh and his new Israel. The record is of the highest importance: first, because it marks the beginning of a distinctively Hebraic cultural symbolism and, secondly, because it gives a quite definite witness to the vital connection between the covenant and the sacrifice. This does not mean, indeed, that the origin of the institution of sacrifice is to be found in this incident. Both the idea of the covenant and the praxis of the sacrifice can be traced back to a far more distant past and, as we have noted, there seems to be a clear connection between the two in the case of the covenant with Abraham. What it does mean, however, is that from now onwards in the life of Israel the covenant and the sacrifice are indissolubly bound together. Only through sacrifice could the covenant be renewed and deepened; every offering of sacrifice was, at least ideally, a witness to the original covenant. So it came about that ultimately, as Bishop F. C. N. Hicks declares in his valuable study of the sacrificial idea:

> " The whole course of the sacrifices [i.e., in Israel] was regarded as belonging to the covenant system. . . . Each kind in its different way was a method of restoring, acknowledging or renewing and enjoying the covenant relationship. Sacrifice was, in fact, to the Jewish mind an essential feature of a covenant. To the modern mind a bond or agreement seems to have no imaginable connection with sacrifice; but if the ancient system is to be understood, it must be realized that when a Jew thought of a covenant, he thought of a sacrifice." [2]

Yet when this has been said, the question still remains whether the whole of the sacrificial system as later developed within Israel was a true development of the original covenant idea. This is a complex and difficult subject and one that cannot be treated in detail here. Suffice it to say that in the writer's view a great deal of the later Jewish system — especially that connected with the sin offering and the guilt offering — while it may not have been a wholly false development was certainly a dangerous one and one that was not necessarily included in the original connection between covenant and sacrifice. Far too much emphasis came to be laid on the sacrifices effecting a quasi-physical purification and renewal of life within the covenant. It is our view that the covenant *was* repaired and renewed through participation in the covenant-sacrifice, but that there was always danger when these effects came to be regarded dominantly from the physical angle rather than from the metaphysical and moral. And later Judaism was ever in peril of surrendering itself to this false outlook.

This leads us to another vexed question about which there has been much discussion and of which again we cannot speak in detail. It concerns the attitude of the prophets to the sacrificial system and whereas there have been those who have claimed that the prophets were altogether opposed to it in every shape or form, others have urged that they were willing to allow its continuance if performed in the right spirit. Both of these answers, we believe, are incomplete. Undoubtedly they were deeply concerned about the obvious abuses which they saw around them and at times gave the impression of wanting to do away with the system *in toto*. But what was their attitude on the more positive side? We believe that the whole record of Jewish prophecy suggests that they stood in the tradition of dramatic symbolism [3] which is so vividly portrayed in the narrative of Ex., ch. 24. Sacrifice in the way in which it is recorded there they were willing to accept; sacrifice that tended to concentrate upon material substance and automatic efficacy they constantly resisted. Thus it was not only the spirit of the worshippers that was the crucial test: it was the question of whether the symbolism of the sacrifices was dominantly moral in its implications or dominantly physical. It is the former type which is, we believe, so clearly revealed in Ex., ch. 24, and this constitutes its importance as a norm for the truly prophetic type of sacrifice in the Bible.

II

In the critical period of Israel's history succeeding the Exile, the sacrificial system largely broke down and those in captivity tended to adopt different attitudes as they looked forward to the re-establishment of the covenant. All were united in their confidence that someday the covenant would be restored and that this would result in the uplift and renewal of their whole national life. But as to *how* this would happen, opinions differed widely.

On the one side, there were those who thought that it would come about through an elaboration and amplification of the sacrificial system. They could claim the authority of such a writer as Ezekiel to support their view and after the return from captivity the attempt was made to carry it into effect by Nehemiah and Ezra and their school of thought. It was at this time, apparently, that the Day of Atonement ceremonies were instituted and the attempt made to renew the covenant annually and repair the breaches through sacrifice. Thus in priestly circles the hope was continually entertained that through strict observance of the Temple ritual, national regeneration would at length come to pass. On the other side there were those who paid little attention to ceremonial sacrifice. Instead they sought to live in the spirit of Jeremiah's great prophecy of the new covenant which would be written inwardly by God and confirmed in the unbroken fellowship between himself and his people.

Against this background of tradition and hope we are able the better to understand Jesus' own reference to covenant and sacrifice. It may at once be asserted with confidence that he did not accept either of the more extreme views just outlined. There is no evidence that he rejected sacrifice altogether but at the same time there is little likelihood that he was content with the sacrificial system as he found it. What seems almost certain is that he identified himself with his people's hope of the new covenant but that he envisaged this as only procurable through the sacrifice of *himself. By pouring out his life in death, the covenant would be repaired, and those participating by faith in the covenant relationship would be renewed and strengthened with the life of the divine.*

Within the actual life and ministry of Jesus, there are few sayings which bear a definitely sacrificial reference. Vincent Taylor [4] has examined with great care all that might bear a suggestiveness of this kind and his results are of much interest. Some of the most notable are the references to the cup and the baptism in Mark 10:38, and the striking words about the fire in Luke 12:49. Moreover, there is the impressive saying in John 17:19 where Jesus speaks of sanctifying himself on behalf of his disciples. The term ' sanctify ' is apparently a sacrificial term, and, after examining its significance, Sir Edwyn Hoskyns decides that by using it in this context, Jesus revealed that he was dedicating himself as a sacrifice in order that his disciples might be sanctified thereby.[5] But these are only suggestive: the passage of altogether outstanding importance in this connection is the record of the Last Supper, and it is that which deserves careful consideration.

We have reserved until now a more detailed exposition of Ex., ch. 24, in order to place it immediately alongside the story of the institution of the new covenant by Jesus. The parallelism in the order and significance of the events is, we believe, quite remarkable. The Exodus story falls into two main sections.

1. Following upon the verbal proclamation of the Law and the verbal declaration of obedience by the people, Moses wrote the words of the Lord in a book, and then proceeded to the dramatic ratification. First an altar was builded under the hill and twelve pillars set up around it to represent the twelve

tribes of Israel. Then young men were commissioned to offer burnt offerings and sacrifice peace offerings unto the Lord while Moses reserved to himself the solemn manipulation of the blood. It is to be noted particularly that the sacrifices offered were of two types: the burnt offerings were wholly consumed in the fire, the peace offerings were in part consumed but in part were given to the worshippers for their consumption. Thus the symbolism appears to be that the costly gifts of the people were all consigned to the fire, some thereby to be made over entirely to God, some to be purified and returned to the people for their nourishment. In other words, through the agency of the fire, Yahweh and his people were enabled to share the substance of the *flesh* and to be thereby strengthened and renewed in their life of mutual relationship.

2. In the second part of the ceremony, half of the blood was first sprinkled on the altar, the object which symbolized the presence of the Deity. Then, after the people had pledged themselves to obedience to the terms of the covenant, the other half was sprinkled upon them. " Behold," says Moses, " the blood of the covenant, which the Lord hath made with you." Thus the symbolism appears to be that through the blood, representing life which has passed through death, the life both of Yahweh and his people was renewed. They were henceforward bound together in a sacred common life, through the agency of the *blood* of the sacrifice. In other words, both God and his worshippers were united together within a new economy which had been made possible through the life voluntarily offered to him.

We now compare this with the account of the Last Supper. Again there are two parts.

1. First a table was prepared and twelve places were assigned to those representative of the new Israel. Then Jesus himself took the loaf, consecrated it to God, gave part to them,[6] and said, " Take, eat; this is my body." No animal was

offered on this occasion. Jesus was himself the sacrifice, his body being symbolized by the bread which he broke in this way. Through his passage through the fire of suffering and death, his life was offered to God and also to his people. God and men could now share a common life in his consecrated body.

2. After supper he took the cup of wine,[7] symbolizing his blood outpoured. Again he consecrated it to God and then gave to his disciples with the command that they should drink it.[8] "This is my blood of the new testament," he said, "which is shed for many." In partaking of the cup, they could share in the new economy made possible through his life surrendered to death.

There are many difficulties connected with the four accounts of the Last Supper, but we believe that the altogether important symbolism which it portrays (thereby establishing a distinctively Christian symbolism in contrast to the Jewish cultural tradition) is substantially as indicated above. To use Dr. H. Wheeler Robinson's expressive phrase, it was "Calvary anticipated in miniature."[9] Jesus voluntarily offered himself to God and invited men to share in his self-offering; God and man were brought into communion in the self-oblation of Christ. Similarly he poured out his life in death and invited men to share in the fruit of his sacrifice; God and man were sealed in their communion together by the self-outpouring of Christ. Without pressing too far the distinction between the body offered and the blood outpoured, it is possible to see in the dual symbolism the suggestion of the flesh and blood which constituted a whole man, being, in the case of Christ, consecrated unreservedly to God. By the strong emotive power of this symbolism, those who were incorporated within the new covenant were ' bound ' to offer themselves, flesh and blood, without stint or reserve, to the service and obedience

of God. And the high importance of the Christian Eucharist
is that on each occasion of its celebration, the covenant is renewed by the dramatic representation of that prophetic sacrifice which Jesus gave as a norm to his Church. Surely the
symbolism of the Supper (especially as expounded in John,
ch. 6) testifies to the fact that Jesus regarded his coming
death as a consecration of humanity to God through his own
self-offering and the creation of their new life in full communion with God by means of his own life passing through
the agony of death.[10] Consecration and communion within
the new covenant are, we believe, the results which Jesus expected to achieve through his suffering and death.

III

Two things only need be said of Jesus' own conception of
his person which corresponds to this aspect of his activity. In
the first place, it is wholly probable that Jesus regarded himself as fulfilling in his own person the prophecy of Mal. 3:1:
" Behold, I will send my messenger, and he shall prepare the
way before me: and the Lord, whom ye seek, shall suddenly
come to his temple, even the messenger of the covenant, whom
ye delight in: behold, he shall come, saith the Lord of hosts."
There is no doubt that in the earliest Christian tradition the
first part of the prophecy was regarded as referring to John
the Baptist and there is good reason to believe that Jesus regarded the second part as referring to himself. Few incidents
in his ministry were planned with such deliberation and executed with such intensity as the cleansing of the Temple. By
this action, Jesus was concerned to show that animal sacrifice
was at an end and that a new covenant was about to be established. He himself was to be the messenger of the covenant,

the new Moses who would act as mediator of the new covenant and bring his people to offer themselves unto the Lord an offering in righteousness (Mal. 3:3).

In the second place, it is clear that Jesus regarded himself in a certain sense as a priest but this sense needs to be carefully defined. One clue is to be found in the comparison of the two narratives to which we have already referred: just as Moses performed priestly functions, though he was not a member of the strict Levitical priesthood, so Jesus was, if we may coin the term, the Prophet-Priest, performing the new act of prophetic symbolism. The other clue is to be found in the unusual incident recorded in Mark 12:35 *seq.* Whatever may have been Jesus' motive in quoting the passage from Ps. 110, he clearly viewed the psalm as a whole as Messianic. And although, as we saw earlier, it is altogether unlikely that Jesus was prepared to accept the Messianic designation under the current form, it *is* probable that by referring to this psalm he was implicitly accepting the two names of ' Lord ' and ' Priest ' which were assigned to the Messiah in it. But to what kind of priest does the psalm refer? Not to the Levitical priesthood, although there was a school of thought within Judaism that looked for a Messiah of strict Levitical descent.

" The Lord hath sworn, and will not repent,
    Thou art a priest for ever
    After the order of Melchizedek ":

Is this not a clear indication that Jesus regarded himself as the new Melchizedekian Priest-King, who would, like his great prototype, bring forth bread and wine (Gen. 14:18) for the refreshing and strengthening of the people of God?

But not only was he the Priest; he was also the Victim. Although there is no definite terminology to which we can appeal, the whole tenor of his life marks him out as a burnt offering, wholly consecrated to God, and as a peace offering, giving renewal of life to his people. He is Mediator of the covenant — he actually *is* the Covenant for he is God's Word to man. He is the Priest directing the sacrifice — he actually *is* the Sacrifice for he is man's true word of consecration to God. In him, God and man are at one.

IV

As we pass on to the later part of the New Testament, we find that the use of the sacrificial metaphor in relation to our Lord's death is not common. Probably the main reason for this was the fact that very few of the early converts were drawn from priestly circles, and within the synagogues the centre of interest was the Law rather than the sacrifice. In The Acts, there is just one reference to the Abrahamic covenant but there are none to the sacrificial system; and apart from references to the Passover Lamb, there are few suggestions of sacrifice in other writings which bear witness to early Christian belief. It is altogether possible that this dearth of material should be offset by the covenant-sacrifice imagery associated with the Christian Eucharist; but, except in the writings of Paul, there is no explicit reference to this in the early documents.

In the case of Paul the situation is a little different, though even in his epistles there are only occasional allusions. The eucharistic teaching in I Cor., chs. 10; 11 is of great interest, bearing definite witness as it does to the ideas of consecration and communion in connection with the Lord's death and resurrection. Paul compares and contrasts the table of the Lord with the altar of the devils; communion with Christ with communion with devils; the cup of the Lord with the cup of devils. There is, he implies, a superficial comparison between the two. Far greater, however, is the contrast; for it was actual

F

communion with God himself that was established through the cross, and this is renewed at every season of communion of the body and blood of Christ. Further, the whole point of his appeal to what happened on the night of the betrayal was to shame the Corinthians out of their gross selfishness and worldliness, the very opposites of consecration and communion. How utterly unworthy these were of the spirit of Him who offered his own body and blood to God and through God to others! Paul's mention of the covenant in this connection would suggest that the association of the Lord's Supper with covenantal and sacrificial ideas was a good deal more common than might be imagined at first sight. As often as they ate the bread and drank the wine they recalled the covenant and yielded themselves afresh to God and entered afresh into the blessed relationship which it had made possible.

Apart from the eucharistic passages and the striking appeal for a true spirit of consecration comparable to Christ's in Eph. 5:2, the main sacrificial metaphor in Paul's writings is to be found in his references to ' blood.' Even this is normally used as a vivid means of recalling the stark realism of the cross but in one instance, Rom. 3:25, the reference to the sacrificial system is more likely. This is the one occasion in all of Paul's writings when he draws his imagery from the expiatory offerings of the Old Testament. " God set forth Christ as a means of expiation," he says; just as, in the view of the priestly writers, a sin offering was effective in cleansing away breaches of the covenant and restoring it to its true efficacy, so, in the view of Paul, the death of Christ acted as a sin offering to cleanse away the sins which had been committed aforetime and passed over by God. Such a use of sacrificial imagery is unique in Paul's writings and is, we judge, to be interpreted in an illustrative way with regard to a particular point and not as establishing a complete parallel between the death of Christ and the expiatory cultus. The same, we believe, is largely true of the references to propitiation (*hilasmos*) in The First Epistle of John. The writer is concerned to show that those within the Christian community who are conscious of sin can be assured of its removal through the blood or expiation of Christ. There is no attempt on his part to explain: he is simply making the confident assertion that whereas, under the Jewish system, breaches of the ritual law could be expiated by the sacrifice of animals, under the Christian economy breaches of the law of love can be expiated through the living effective action of Christ as he applies to believers the blood of his cross.

The only place in the New Testament where the covenant-sacrifice idea is worked out in detail is in The Epistle to the Hebrews. There are many problems connected with this epistle and the book is far from easy to summarize. One of its most remarkable features is its emphasis upon the imperfection and even the failure of Judaism and upon the sharp contrast which exists between the Jewish system and the Christian faith. Nowhere is this contrast more marked than in the author's conception of the two covenants. First, he fastens upon the covenant made with Israel at Sinai and dwells upon the various ordinances and institutions which it established. There was the tabernacle and the priesthood and the whole sacrificial system; but none of these, the author claims, were able to sanctify the worshippers or bring them into fellowship with God. This was a system which depended upon a changeable priesthood and an earthly sanctuary and animal sacrifices. Such a system, he declares, was effete and outworn and ready to vanish away.

Yet although there seems in all this to be a certain lack of sympathy with all that was of positive value in the Jewish system, there can be no doubt that by means of this sharp contrast the author is able to set forth the excellence of the new covenant in the clearest possible light. Into the very midst of the old order, Jesus himself came. Identifying himself with his brethren, tempted in all points as they were, he was no mere official but one able to represent his brethren truly in the presence of God. But in order that the new covenant might actually come into being, it was necessary that a death should take place. Why exactly this was so, the author does not perhaps make clear but regards it as in some way self-evident. A death was necessary to redeem from transgressions committed under the old covenant, the shedding of blood was necessary to provide cleansing from sin, a testator's death was necessary to bring any new testament into operation. Finally he clinches the matter by an appeal to the covenant of Ex., ch. 24, and to the way in which Christ has fulfilled all these foreshadowings by his own death and endless life.

Often the details of the author's argument are hard to follow but certain of his main ideas stand out clearly. He was a man of vivid imagination who saw the living reality of the Christian order in strongest possible contrast to the shadowy impermanence of the Jewish régime. An earthly temple with successive generations of imperfect priests offering continually the same sacrifices made little appeal to him. But over against this he saw Jesus, the one perfect High Priest, offering a unique sacrifice, even the sacrifice of himself, once for all (Heb. 10:10, 14). He saw him, too, passing into the heavenly sanctuary there to minister continually and effectively on behalf of his people, delivering them from the burden of their sins and bringing them into a true communion with God himself. The new covenant seemed so splendid, so manifestly superior, that the old faded into insignificance. In certain respects — the emphasis on purging by blood, the emphasis on the details of the tabernacle and its furniture, the emphasis on priesthood — there seems to be a difference from the rest of the New Testament. At the same time, in his insistence that by the self-offering of Christ in death a new covenant was established; in his further insistence that all those within the covenant relationship could enjoy a new fellowship with God in the power of the endless life of their great High Priest, the author is entirely in accord with the teaching of the Gospels and his book provides an outstanding example of the use of the covenant-sacrifice metaphor in the interpretation of the significance of the death of Christ.

V

Finally we need only call attention to the fact that Jesus is called both Mediator and High Priest in the latest documents of the Bible. In I Tim. 2:5 and again in Heb. 9:15, the term 'mediator' occurs but it is not a popular title, possibly again because of the lack of priestly associations in the New Testament. The more important title is that of 'high priest' which occurs so frequently in The Epistle to the Hebrews, and makes a further link with Ps. 110. Jesus, says the writer, was called of God, a high priest after the order of Melchizedek; having been called, he was disciplined in the fire of suffering and agony of spirit and prepared for his supreme self-offering; finally, he became the cause of eternal salvation to all who surrendered themselves to him (Heb. 5:8–10). How great this Melchizedekian High Priest was! No effort is spared to set forth his high dignity. Yet how lowly he was! "A body hast thou prepared me. . . . Lo, I come to do thy will, O God." High Priest—Victim; Consecrator—Consecrated: such is the Christ of the New Testament. In him we are separated from evil and consecrated to God; in him we are raised above all that is merely temporal and brought into fellowship with the Eternal. The Christ who is Saviour and Vindicator is also the Sanctifier: through him, we 'draw near' to God.

5. The Cross in the New Testament —
Forgiveness and Reconciliation

"I am crucified with Christ: nevertheless I live; yet not I, but Christ liveth in me: and the life which I now live in the flesh I live by the faith of the Son of God, who loved me, and gave himself for me."   — Gal. 2:20.

I

Three formative ideas of the Jewish people have so far been considered: the redemption from Egypt, the rule of Yahweh, and the covenant of Sinai. It would be hard to exaggerate the influence which these basic concepts had upon all the later life and thought of Judaism. At the same time, there was one more general concept which seems to have occupied an important place in the national consciousness even before the time of the deliverance from Egypt: this was the strong sense of being the descendants of one notable ancestor, Abraham. There were different tribes and different families in Israel but all were conscious of belonging to the one great family of which Abraham had been the recognized head.

This awareness of a common ancestry sends us back to the Genesis records where Abraham was promised a numerous and prosperous progeny: " I will make of thee a great nation, and I will bless thee, and make thy name great; . . . and in thee shall all families of the earth be blessed " (Gen. 12:2, 3) . " And I will make thy seed as the dust of the earth: so that if a man can number the dust of the earth, then shall thy seed also be numbered " (Gen. 13:16) . In addition, Abraham was promised the land of Canaan as his family home: " Unto thy seed will I give this land: . . . and I will

give unto thee, and to thy seed after thee, the land wherein
thou art a stranger " (Gen. 12:7; 17:8) . A seed and a home —
these were the great promises to Abraham. But the promise
did not cease with Abraham. In Gen. 28:13, 14, when Jacob
was going forth into the great unknown, the promise was renewed to him: " I am the Lord God of Abraham thy father,
and the God of Isaac: the land whereon thou liest, to thee will
I give it, and to thy seed; and thy seed shall be as the dust of
the earth."

These promises tended at times to become obscured but
they were never wholly forgotten. God had chosen out Abraham, had constituted him the head of a great family, and had
pledged to him a permanent home. This relationship between God and Abraham was different from that existing
between other peoples and their gods for they had grown up
in a particular environment and had made the Baal of the
land their god. In the case of Israel, however, God had definitely intervened: he had chosen a man and made him the
head of his people and in a special way; therefore, Israel was
God's family. In course of time, the group inclined to accom-
modate itself to the practices of other tribes around it, but in
periods of crisis the old family feeling re-asserted itself, usually through the words of a particular leader. Thus the terms
of Moses' initial commission included a command to say to
the people that the Lord God of their fathers, the God of
Abraham, Isaac and Jacob, had sent him to them (Ex. 3:15)
and that he would lead them to the land of their desire, the
land flowing with milk and honey. To Pharaoh, Moses was
commanded to say, " Israel is my son, even my first-born: and I
say unto thee, Let my son go, that he may serve me " (Ex.
4:22, 23) . Here we see the backward look to the common
ancestry, which derived ultimately from God's call, and the
forward look to the delectable land, which was included
within God's promise.

As we have already suggested, the great danger which was ever threatening the life of Israel was that it would lose its distinctive character through absorption into the paganism of the surrounding peoples. It was against this danger in its many forms that the words of the prophets were mainly directed. They saw Israel turning away from God, seeking its satisfaction in other ways, acting as a disloyal and rebellious son or as an unfaithful and pleasure-loving wife, and by every means in their power they sought to bring home to the nation the enormity of its sin and yet the patience of the forgiving heart of Yahweh. Two of the earliest prophets were Amos and Hosea and each of these appealed to imagery drawn from family relationships in order to move the hearts of their hearers towards repentance.

In the prophecy of Amos, the first two chapters are devoted to an exposure of the sins of Judah and Israel and of the tribes which surrounded them. In practically every case, the sins specified are outrages against common humanity, unbrotherly conduct, offences against the basic relationships of life. Then at the beginning of the third chapter the prophet gathers all together in a single denunciation of the ' whole family ' which had been brought up from the land of Egypt. " You only," says Yahweh, " have I known of all the families of the earth: therefore I will punish you for all your iniquities " (Amos 3:2). In other words, to be a chosen family does not simply involve privilege; rather, it involves a unique responsibility, and it is in Israel's failure to fulfil that responsibility that its greatest sin lies.

A similar emphasis is to be found in the prophecy of Hosea, though in terms of imagery even more dramatic than that of Amos. For behind this book there lies a story of personal tragedy as poignant as any in the Old Testament. Hosea had taken a wife to himself in absolute love and trust; she had borne him children; and then, to his utter dismay, she had proved unfaithful. She descended to the lowest form of degradation and might have been regarded as beyond reclaim. Yet Hosea sought her out, bought her in the market place, released her from her shame and probably restored her ultimately to her full conjugal rights. In all this, Hosea sees a vivid picture of Yahweh's treatment of Israel. Though the parallelism need not be stressed in every detail, it is the land, or even we might say the state, which is regarded as the wife of Yahweh, and successive generations of the people are the children of the marriage. The earlier part of the book tends to speak in more general terms of the apostasy of the land from its overlord, of the state from its husband. The second part, however, speaks in more personal terms of the disloyalty of children who have turned away from the Father who loved them, and the picture comes to its full expression in ch. 11, where, in passages of great beauty, Yahweh is portrayed as a father loving his children, calling them to himself, taking them by the arms and teaching them to walk. Even when they begin to turn away, the father continues to love them and refuses to give them up: " How shall I give thee up, Ephraim? how shall I deliver thee, Israel? . . . O Israel, thou hast destroyed thyself; but in me is thine help." So speaks the Love that will not let them go and ultimately it breaks forth into a passionate cry: " O Israel, return unto the Lord thy God. . . . Take with you words, and turn to the Lord. . . . I will heal their backsliding, I will love them freely. . . . I will be as the dew unto Israel." Nowhere in the Old Testament is the parental love of Yahweh more vividly set forth; yet nowhere perhaps in the Old Testament does a man more fully enter into the costliness of hearing and proclaiming the word of the Lord.

In the years succeeding the Exile, two of the main developments in the life of Israel were fostered, on the one side by those devoted to the ritual law, on the other side by those given up to the pursuit of wisdom; and within these two movements, strongly contrasted views were held regarding the relations of Israel with the neighbouring peoples. In a general sense, both groups desired that men should know God and love him, but whereas this led the former group to strive for an exclusive family which could truly be regarded as God's elect children, it led the latter to adopt an attitude of widely inclusive benevolence, regarding the best of men everywhere as beloved of God.

The clearest examples of the former attitude may be seen in the books of Ezra and Nehemiah, records which became in a large measure formative for later thought. The supreme object of these two leaders was to bring into existence a community which should be racially pure, a new seed as it were, a regenerated family. To this end they introduced a policy of complete separation. The essence of the people's sin is defined in striking words: " They have taken of their [i.e., foreigners'] daughters for themselves, and for their sons: so that the holy seed have mingled themselves with the people of those lands: yea, the hand of the princes and rulers hath been chief in this trespass " (Ezra 9:2). This is the burden which Ezra took upon himself as he confessed the people's sins before God; and the outcome was that " the seed of Israel separated themselves from all strangers, and stood and confessed their sins " (Neh. 9:2). So strong was this feeling towards racial purity that it became almost an obsession in later Judaism: only by cutting themselves off from every contact with heathenism, they believed, could they constitute themselves the chosen family, the holy seed after God's own heart.

On the other side the Wisdom writers both of the Old Testament and of the apocryphal literature tended to adopt an attitude which might well be described as ' international humanism.' [1] There was little attempt, at least in the earlier Wisdom writings, to confine the favour of God exclusively to Israel, and there was a notable insistence upon the obligations which were laid upon all men by reason of their participation in a common humanity. Moreover, there was a vivid sense of God's overruling providence which was not confined to any one people or nation. " It is in the Wisdom literature both of Israel and Egypt with its inherent interest in humanity that the idea of a divine providence presiding over each individual person reaches its fullest development, and appears in every respect to be on a level with the New Testament assurance that the very hairs of man's head are numbered." [2] This thought comes to perhaps its most beautiful expression in The Wisdom of Solomon (ch. 11:23 *seq.*) :

> " Thou hast mercy on all men, because thou hast power
> to do all things,
> And thou overlookest the sins of men to the end they
> may repent.
> For thou lovest all things that are,
> And abhorrest none of the things which thou didst
> make;
> For never wouldest thou have formed anything if
> thou didst hate it. . . .
> But thou sparest all things, because they are thine.
> O Sovereign Lord, thou lover of men's lives;
> For thine incorruptible spirit is in all things " (R.V.).

It would be hard to find a loftier conception of God's universal family, and yet it suffers from a grave defect. " Thou overlookest the sins of men " is not enough as it stands. The extreme emphasis on separation from purely physical contamination may be bad enough on one side, but it is equally dangerous on the other side to assume that " *Dieu pardonnera? C'est son métier.*" Blandly to argue that all the world is God's family, within the ambit of his love, and that that is all that need be said, is to shut oneself up within a pitiful in-difference to the real needs of the world.

Thus some other message was needed to reveal to men the nature of God's Fatherhood and the character of the family that he desired to have. There is, we believe, the framework of such a message in the writings of the prophets. Jeremiah looks forward to the day when the Lord will be God of all the families of Israel and they shall be his people. It was in the far land that he had appeared saying, " Yea, I have loved thee with an everlasting love: therefore with lovingkindness have I drawn thee " (Jer. 31:3). The Second Isaiah also proclaims to the people: " Fear not: for I am with thee: I will bring thy seed from the east, and gather thee from the west; I will say to the north, Give up; and to the south, Keep not back: bring my sons from far, and my daughters from the ends of the earth (Isa. 43:5, 6). " I will bring forth a seed out of Jacob, and out of Judah an inheritor of my mountains: and mine elect shall inherit it, and my servants shall dwell there " (Isa. 65:9). Thus in a real sense the hope of the second part of Isaiah's prophecy centres in a restored family, a new seed, a home in which sons and daughters will live joyfully together in trust and loyalty towards their Father-God. It was this hope which in Jesus Christ became reality.

II

We have seen in previous chapters that the Gospel of Mark bears clear witness in its early sections to Jesus' consciousness of the struggle in which he was engaged and of the Kingdom which he was to establish. At the end of the third chapter, however, appears another significant idea which demands our attention. Up to this stage, most of the utterances of Jesus have been set in the midst of healing-stories or of records of

controversy. But now a section of the Gospel is devoted to a
different kind of utterance: there is more intimate teaching,
teaching by parables, and this is directed not only to his disciples but to all who are interested enough to draw near and
hear the word of God.

The section opens with a picture of a group surrounding
Jesus and listening attentively to his words. Suddenly there is
a disturbance on the edge of the crowd, for members of Jesus'
own family are anxious to draw near and talk with him.
News of this is brought to Jesus and elicits from him a
remarkable saying. No longer can the natural ties of home
and mother and family bind him. He is creating a new family whose members are joined together by ties of a different
kind. " He looked round about on them which sat about him,
and said, Behold my mother and my brethren! For whosoever
shall do the will of God, the same is my brother and my sister, and mother " (Mark 3:34, 35) . In commenting on this
saying, Dr. R. N. Flew remarks that " where Mark writes ' whosoever shall do the will of God,' Luke transcribes ' these which
hear the word of God and do it.' This is true interpretation." [3]
In other words, we should be justified in saying that Jesus included within his new family (which he must have regarded
as the family of God, the true Israel) all who were prepared
to open their ears and respond with their hearts to the word
of God which he proclaimed.

In the Gospel story, the immediate sequel to this incident is
the group of parables dealing with the seed, and it is of interest to recall the fact that seed used in the fields was most
closely connected in men's minds with the seed of the human
body.[4] Thus there may have already existed in Jesus' thoughts
a subtle connection between the seed of the Word sown in
the hearts of men and bearing its harvest in their lives and the
seed of the divine life, reproducing itself in the world and
bringing into being the new family of God. His Word was

the new proclamation which would bring forth fruit in human hearts unto life eternal; his living Spirit was the new
seed which would mysteriously germinate and gather together
a new family sustained by the very life of God. This process
was going on even in the days of his flesh, but the time would
come when an event would happen bearing still greater consequences for mankind. " Except a corn of wheat fall into
the ground and die, it abideth alone: but if it die, it bringeth forth much fruit " (John 12:24). The Word himself must
pass through the experience of death and rise to become the
message of salvation for the whole world: he who was the
Light of life must go down into the darkness of the grave and
rise to become the glory illuminating all mankind. *Thus
whereas through Jesus' life and teaching the new family was
beginning to be formed, it was only through his suffering and
death that God's holy and universal family could finally come
into existence.* Each of these aspects must now be considered
in rather fuller detail.

If we begin by asking what was the heart of the new revelation which Jesus made to this inner circle of his hearers, there
can be no doubt at all about the answer. The supreme revelation was the profoundly simple one that God was their Father. This was by no means a new thought but there was
nothing in the Old Testament to compare with the compre-
hensiveness and the intimacy of Jesus' presentation of this
great truth. He did not begin with any attempt to gather together men of superior race or culture: in fact the Galileans
who formed the immediate circle around him were regarded
by the Jewish leaders as of doubtful social status and as devoid of any knowledge of higher things. But Jesus was prepared to receive within his circle all who were prepared to
listen to the word of God. He constituted them a family and
began to tell them of the character of their Father.[5]

What, then, were the main emphases in Jesus' disclosure of

the character of God to his inner circle? We suggest that there were two, although it might justly be claimed that in the last resort these are not two but one.

1. A proclamation of the fact that God forgives his own children unreservedly but calls upon them, in a similar way, to forgive their brethren within the family, whatever their offences towards them may be.

2. A revelation of the fact that God loves his own children ceaselessly but calls upon them to show forth a similar spirit of love in all their relations with one another.

Let us take first the subject of forgiveness. In Mark, the only reference to forgiveness in Jesus' talks to his inner circle is in ch. 11:25. " And when ye stand praying, forgive, if ye have ought against any: that your Father also which is in heaven may forgive you your trespasses." In Matthew there are the well-known words of the Lord's Prayer and the answer to Peter's question concerning the number of times that it was desirable and necessary to forgive an erring brother. This answer leads on to the parable of the Unforgiving Servant, the story which most fully expresses Jesus' teaching on the subject to his inner circle of followers. These are all the direct references, though in the Sermon on the Mount, for example, there are repeated appeals for a generous and forgiving spirit in all dealings with the other members of the family. Thus the teaching might be summarized as follows: There are no limits to the Father's forgiveness (in the parable the debt is really beyond computation) ; there should therefore be no limits to the children's forgiveness either. To shut one's heart against a brother, to harbour a grudge or a secret enmity, is to cut oneself off entirely from true membership of the family of God.[6]

Turning then to the subject of God's unfailing love, one of the most striking passages is the sixth chapter of Matthew and certain sections of the seventh. The recurring refrain is simply, " Thy Father . . . seeth," " Your . . . Father knoweth," " Your . . . Father feedeth," " Shall your Father . . . give? " Men need not fear to perform acts of devotion in secret: the Father sees and remembers. Men need not fear concerning life and food and clothing: the Father knows their needs. Men need not fear to ask with boldness and confidence: the Father gives good gifts to those who ask him. Nothing could more fully express the love of the Father for his children; the only thing that can prevent them from experiencing that love to the full is a lack of trust in his good will towards them and a failure to manifest the same spirit of love in their relations with their fellow men.

Thus, in Jesus' teaching there was the constant dual emphasis upon the unqualified forgiveness of the Father and the ceaseless outpouring of his love. But not only was this true of his teaching: it was equally true of his life. The Word through his message, the Spirit through his life, were one and the same. Yet it is impossible to read the Gospels without the consciousness that in Jesus' view even that was not enough. The same Word must be spoken through his suffering and death; the same Spirit must be revealed. Only so could the family circle be extended to its fullest limits. This fact is set forth in a strangely ironical way in the Fourth Gospel. The Evangelist is commenting on the callous words of Caiaphas whereby he judged that it was expedient for one man to die for the people. " And this spake he not of himself: but being high priest that year, he prophesied that Jesus should die for that nation; and not for that nation only, but that also he should *gather together in one the children of God* that were scattered abroad " (John 11:51, 52). Similarly, arising out of the request of the Greeks to see Jesus, there comes first the parable of the Death of the Seed, and this leads on to the final triumph-cry of Jesus, " And I, if I be lifted up from the earth, will draw all men unto me " (John 12:32). In his lifting-up in death and resurrection, he would so reveal the forgiveness and love of God as to draw together all the scattered children of God into one family around himself.

How, then, was this final proclamation to be made? May we not first hear it in the words of forgiveness spoken out of the midst of the most unjust and cruel treatment that could be inflicted upon a son of man? One of his disciples betrayed him with a kiss: he still called him ' friend.' The other disciples forsook him and fled: he still called them his brethren. No word of bitterness was addressed to his captors or judges, and when finally the soldiers nailed him to the cross, the sublimest expression of forgiveness of all time issued from his lips: " Father, forgive them; for they know not what they do." It was a double proclamation: the outreach of the divine forgiveness was proclaimed; the possible response in human forgivingness was likewise proclaimed. No man need ever despair of the forgiveness of God; no man need ever reach a limit beyond which forgiveness to others could not be given.

And what of the final revelation? It is seen surely in the love which shines forth from the midst of utter darkness — love towards a dying bandit, love towards a sorrowing mother and friend, love towards the daughters of Jerusalem typifying suffering humanity, a love which does not turn away from sin and sorrow and despair but having loved His own in the world, loves to the end. It is seen too in the trust which remains stedfast through every test and trial. " He trusted in God," cried the passers-by; and unwittingly they uttered words of profoundest truth. He trusted in God, believing that neither life nor death nor any other created thing could separate him from the love of God. So it was a double revelation: the divine love was revealed in all its fulness; the possible response in human trust was likewise revealed. No man need ever stand outside the love of God; no man need ever reach a point where trust in God becomes impossible. Thus in Jesus

G

— his words, his life, his death and resurrection — the Word of forgiveness was spoken, the Spirit of love was revealed, and the new family of God came into being. He saw " of the travail of his soul " (Isa. 53:11) and was satisfied, for a new life was born into the world, the life of the beloved children of God.

III

Turning now to the titles, we find that although there are in the Gospels two veiled allusions to Jesus as the Bridegroom, these are altogether exceptional. The name by which Jesus represented the ' family ' aspect of his saving work was in almost every instance ' Son of God ' or simply ' the Son.' Moreover, at least in the Synoptic Gospels, this is the name which is used beyond all others in his intimate words to his inner circle of followers. The chief examples can be rapidly surveyed.

As is well known, the term ' son ' in relation to God is used only sparingly in the Old Testament. Israel is referred to as God's son; the king is addressed in like manner: and later, as in Ps. 2:7, the title is applied to the Messiah; but in no case are the implications of the name fully worked out. If, however, we are to accept St. Luke's story at the end of his second chapter, there was a deep filial consciousness in Jesus even in the days of his boyhood, and this consciousness came to overt expression in the dramatic incident of his baptism.[7] Now there is every reason to believe that the intimate revelation of what took place at his baptism and temptation could only have been made to his own inmost circle; the same is certainly true of the transfiguration and the agony of Gethsemane, and in a measure true also of the profound experience recorded in Matt. 11:25–27. The significant thing is that it is in the passages which describe these particular incidents that the name Son is used with a frequency and a meaningfulness found nowhere else in the Synoptic Gospels. It was only in the family circle, as it were, that Jesus was prepared to make himself known as the Son.[8]

This sense of sonship was to be tested through temptations; it was to come to its richest expression in intimate experiences of prayer and communion with God, the most remarkable of which is recorded in Matt. 11:25–27; and it was to receive its final testing through the prevision of the cross which came to him so vividly on the Mount of Transfiguration and in the Garden of Gethsemane. Yet his assurance of Sonship never faltered and his loving identification with his brethren never ceased. All that his Sonship meant to him we can never know. Yet, as Vincent Taylor so well puts it, " The ultimate truth about Jesus is that He is the Son of God. The Synoptic Gospels do not tell us what that title means and the best answers of Christian theology are incomplete. What can be said with confidence is that a filial relationship with the Father, to which there is a parallel nowhere else, is the secret of the ministry and work of Jesus." [9] And we may add as a corollary, it was as the Son that Jesus went to his cross; it was as Son that Jesus suffered and died and rose again; and it follows that unless the whole thing was a tragic illusion and falsehood, it was in the cross supremely that the heart of the Father stood forever revealed.

It is in this revelation of Jesus as the Son of God, a revelation given mainly though not exclusively to his inner circle of disciples, that the heart of the Fourth Gospel lies; [10] and as Son, he was able to give a full revelation of the Father. " It would be easy," writes W. F. Howard, " to multiply examples of the claim that Jesus makes in the Fourth Gospel to unbroken filial unity with the Father. The knowledge which he displays, the marvellous powers which he exercises, are not inherent in Jesus but are given him by the Father. The words which he utters are not his own, but the Father who sent him

has given him commandment what to say. The relationship
is always expressed in personal terms. On the Father's side
there is love and confidence. ' The Father loveth the Son, and
hath given all things into his hand.' On the Son's side the
story reveals love and obedient trust. ' The cup which my
Father hath given me, shall I not drink it? ' The discourse in
the Upper Room with its culmination in the great Prayer sets
forth most fully this profound unity of will and understand-
ing between the Father and the Son." [11] And again it must be
added as a corollary, it was as Son that Jesus went to the cross.
No interpretation of the cross can do it justice which does not
give full weight to the fact that it was the very Son of God
who was suffering and dying there. Doubtless from the human
point of view it was a son of man who was there ' lifted up '
(John 3:14; 8:28) ; but from the divine point of view it was
the Son of God who was there ' glorified.' " God so loved the
world, that he gave his only begotten Son," exalted him in
death and glorified him in life. Whosoever believes that in
the cross the final word of God is spoken, that in the ' glori-
fication ' of the Son the heart of God stands forever revealed,
does not perish but enters into the enjoyment of sonship
which is eternal life.

IV

In the writings of Paul, there are two verbs that serve to
bring out the particular aspect of Christ's work which we
are examining in this chapter. These two verbs are ' forgive '
and ' reconcile,' though the first of these needs to have certain
qualifications attached to it. Two Greek verbs used by Paul
are in our Authorized Version translated ' forgive '; but
whereas the first of these derives its significance from the underlying thought of loosing or setting free,[12] the second has

a more intimate and personal relevance, and it is this latter verb which we must examine in more detail.

The verb *charizomai* is of course intimately associated with the noun *charis* and the two must share the same underlying meaning. Undoubtedly for Paul they expressed, as far as words ever could, the great act of divine self-giving whereby God had given the Son of his love to a world of unlovely and sinful men. Everything, in Paul's view, was derived from the grace of God. No term in his vocabulary was more comprehensive: in it he sought to include the whole of God's self-giving in Christ. When, however, we examine the verb in its contexts, we find that, generally speaking, it refers to a special and particular manifestation of grace. As Dr. Moffatt points out:

> " So vital a part of ' charis ' was forgiveness that Paul required a special verb in this connection. He finally took over *charizesthai* to denote forgiveness, human as well as divine; which was a new departure, for up till now this verb had been confined to giving or bestowing, without reference to moral offences. But as God's gift or gracious boon meant pardon of sins for men, so it was not unnatural that a verb which denoted ' give ' in ordinary language should now mean ' forgive ' as well. . . .
> " What seems to have led Paul to develop this verb was his consciousness of the divine grace in pardon. When he thought ' God gives,' he instinctively thought ' God forgives.' " [13]

Thus, in the verb *charizomai*, we find both an overwhelming sense of the free self-giving of God and an indication that it had come to a particular focus in the limitless forgiveness manifested in Christ.

The important contexts for the examination of this word are II Cor. 2:7–10; Eph. 4:32; Col. 2:13; 3:13. We discover that in every case the context is one of intimate and moving appeal. Paul is writing to friends, to brothers and sisters in the family of God, and he appeals to them to forgive their fellow Christians just as freely, just as generously, as God had forgiven them. In II Cor., ch. 2, for example, a brother had evidently sinned and been separated from the fellowship; punishment had been inflicted and the man had been weighed down by sorrow. Now, however, the apostle appeals for a definite expression of forgiveness: " Instead of censuring you should now forgive him, . . . reinstate him in your love. . . . Anything I had to forgive him has been forgiven in the presence of Christ for your sakes " (vs. 7, 8, 10, Moffatt's Translation). As Christ had expressed the forgiveness of God, so Paul was expressing the forgiveness of Christ and appealing to the Corinthian Christians to express the same forgiveness by inviting the erring brother into their fellowship again. A similar appeal is to be found in each of the other passages. Behind the appeal stands the sublime fact that God, in Christ, freely forgave you: the consequence follows, " Be ye kind . . . , tenderhearted, forgiving one another, . . . even as Christ forgave you, so also do ye." There is, it is true, no specific mention of the cross in the passages though in Col. 2:13 it cannot have been absent from the apostle's mind. The teaching, however, is clear. God, in his whole revelation in Christ, which must have included the cross as its focal point, proclaimed his word of forgiveness to men: they on their part, in all their relationships within the brotherhood, must forgive just as freely and wholeheartedly as God had forgiven them. From all that Paul says of *charis* at other points, we must believe that this forgiving grace of God had been supremely revealed to him in that cross, where the Son of God loved him and gave himself up for him.

Charizomai then is used by Paul in appeals to the inner circle of his fellow Christians, to describe that free forgiveness which is an essential preliminary to the restoration of full fellowship. " The thought is that of the setting aside through love of barriers in the way of fellowship. There is no case in which *charizomai* is used to suggest the full restoration of broken relationships; action leading to this end, and necessary to it, is the meaning implied." [14] What word, then, does Paul use in describing this full restoration to the family relationship? We believe that the word is ' reconciliation,' even though it may not immediately suggest the special relationships which we have in mind. There are four main passages in Paul's writings where it is used and each is worthy of careful consideration: II Cor. 5:18–20; Rom. 5:10–12; Eph. 2:16; and Col. 1:20 *seq*. Without going into details of exegesis [15] we may note certain things which are of interest for our immediate purpose.

In the first place the noun *katallagē* and its corresponding verbs do not of themselves suggest any vivid imagery. Apparently they were originally used in connection with money changing but this fact only gives us the thought of change from one currency to another. In classical Greek they were employed in a quite general sense to denote a change from a state of enmity to one of friendship, the healing of a quarrel: and it is at least worthy of note that this implied the renewal of a relationship of a more intimate and personal kind than that existing between, shall we say, different nations or between individuals having little knowledge of one another. There seems to be the suggestion of real friendship, first existing, then broken, and finally restored. However, the word in itself gives us a bare minimum of suggestion and it is only by reference to the context that this can be amplified.

In the Septuagint Version of the Old Testament, the term is used only twice and neither of the passages offers any real help. In II Maccabees, however, there are several passages where the word occurs. The chief emphasis is upon the fact that God had been angry with his people, for a little while for their ' chastening and correction,' yet he would be reconciled with them again and restore them to prosperity. Passing on to the New Testament, we find that there are just two occasions when the word is not used in a strictly religious context. In the first, Matt. 5:24,[16] ' reconciliation ' is to be between a man and his brother and even though the brother may not be a blood relation, the connection between the two parties is obviously very close. In the second, I Cor. 7:11, the possibility is envisaged that a Christian wife who had departed from her pagan husband might be ' reconciled ' to him; here again the relationship is of the most intimate kind. When we add to these two occurrences of the term the question to an oracle quoted by Moulton and Milligan from the papyri, " Am I to be reconciled with my offspring? " it seems fair to conclude that the noun *katallagē* and its corresponding verbs were normally employed in connection with the healing of breaches between those who had originally been on terms of very close intimacy and friendship.

In the four classic passages referred to above, two ideas emerge which are important for our enquiry: they are ' enmity ' and ' alienation.' In the Romans passage, those who are now reconciled are spoken of as having previously been ' enemies '; in Eph. 2:15, 16 the work of Christ is said to have resulted in the abolition of the ' enmity,' the cross having actually been the means whereby the ' enmity ' was slain; in v. 12 of the same chapter there is a reference to those who were once ' alienated ' from the commonwealth of Israel and strangers from the covenant of promise; and finally in the Colossians passage the two ideas are brought together when it is said that those who had been ' alienated ' and ' enemies ' in their mind had been reconciled by God. Taking these passages together, it is clear that the state previous to reconciliation had been one of ' alienation ' and ' enmity.' What do these two terms mean? As regards the first, Dr. Armitage Robinson comments that Paul, in using this word, seems to have in mind Ps. 69:8, " I became alienated from my brothers and a stranger to the sons of my mother." In other words, ' alienation ' is a term used of estrangement of feeling within the family relationship; those who should be brothers are separated from one another as aliens. With regard to the second, the idea of ' enmity ' has given rise to considerable discussion, especially around the question of whether there was enmity on the side of God or of man or of both. The Colossians passage seems to make it clear that the primary thought in Paul's mind is that of man's hostility towards God. Whereas God's purpose is towards friendship, man remains stubbornly resentful and hostile. This is confirmed by the passage in Rom., ch. 5, where the apostle stresses the fact that *we* were enemies: immediately before, he has spoken of the fact that we were sinners, and the inference seems clear that to be in a state of sin is inevitably to be in a state of hostility towards God. In Ephesians, the ' enmity ' concerns rather the Jew and the Gentile, and the striking claim is made that by his cross Christ had destroyed this old racial antagonism and at the same time had broken down the hostility which both Jew and Gentile felt towards God. In all the references to enmity there seems to be no reference to enemies in battle or to active hostilities between two groups; the whole stress is on feelings of hostility between those who should be bound together by the closest ties of friendship. Thus in summing up what these two ideas suggest concerning the *need* of reconciliation we may with confidence affirm that they view men as separated from their true home, hostile to the Father who loves them and alienated from their brethren with whom they should be living on terms of closest relationship within the same family. The essence of the work of reconciliation was thus the restoring of men to their true relationship as sons and friends of the Heavenly Father and as brothers and friends of one another. Although parental and family relationships are not explicitly mentioned, it seems fair to say that behind the word *katallagē*, there lies a system of relationships best symbolized and represented by those of a human home.

In this section, our main purpose has been to point out the close connections between the words ' forgive ' (*charizomai*) and ' reconcile ' (*katallassō*) on the one side and the complex of metaphors which surround the institution of the home and the family on the other. Within the Christian fellowship, situations were constantly arising which called for a generous spirit of forgiveness and a willingness to make peace. Paul therefore was constantly reminding his readers that their own position within the fellowship was simply due to the forgiveness and reconciliation which God had manifested towards them in Christ: " God in Christ forgave you." " God was in Christ, reconciling the world unto himself." In and through Christ, and supremely in and through his cross, a new word had been spoken, a new spirit had been manifested to the world. Only those who continued to live within the spirit of that cross could enjoy real fellowship with God or with one another; only those who responded to the word of that cross could return from estrangement and alienation to the warmth of the love of the Father's home.

V

In the epistles of Paul, the titles which correspond most closely to the verbs just considered are ' Son of God ' and the anarthrous ' Christ.' These two were evidently almost interchangeable in the apostle's speaking and writing, as may be seen in the classic confessions of Gal. 2:20. " The Son of God . . . loved me, and gave himself for me "; " God commendeth his love toward us, in that, while we were yet sinners, Christ died for us " — these are two outstanding utterances which re-

veal Paul's consciousness that it was in Christ, the Son, that
the love of God had been fully revealed and that that love had
come to its focal expression in the cross of Calvary. He does
not work out a full theology of the cross in terms of sonship
and the restoration of intimate personal fellowship, but he
provides rich material for all those who have since his time
attempted so to do. He knew that he himself had been alienated from God and an enemy in his own mind, but in the Son
he had seen true sonship and by identification with him in
death and resurrection life he had, he believed, been brought
back into the true household of God, not only as a son but as
an heir — an heir of God and a joint-heir with Christ — to
share his sufferings but also to be made partaker of his glory.

In the remainder of the New Testament, the most notable
exposition of the Atonement in terms of family relationships
is to be found in The First Epistle of John. The author is
deeply concerned to make known the nature of true fellowship within the Christian family in contrast to the false ideas
which were being disseminated by Gnostic teachers. He in-
sists that this fellowship is with the Father and with his Son
Jesus Christ, and that it must issue in a genuine love for the
brethren. But inasmuch as sin is never finally eliminated from
the fellowship, he pleads with his readers to walk in the light
of God which shines forth in all its splendour from the cross
of Calvary. Nothing, he believed, could more quickly awaken
souls to shame and penitence than the sight of the outpoured
blood of the Son of God. Through the cross they could be
cleansed from all their sin. But not only so. Through the ministry of the Son (I John 4:10), the Paraclete (ch. 2:1, 2), they
could be fully restored to the Father's fellowship.

In this epistle, then, our Lord figures pre-eminently as ' the
Son,' who dwells in unbroken fellowship with the Father, and
as ' the Paraclete,' who has a perfect knowledge of the Father's
mind. The Son is certainly at one with the Father but he is

also akin to the brethren and so is able to restore them to the full experience of the Father's love. In another sense, however, he is 'Paraclete.' " Originally this relationship was hereditary, and the Advocate was the head of the clan, bound by sacred ties to those whom he served, who might expect his aid whenever public speech and influence were necessary to them or advice in difficult affairs." [17] In other words, he was a kind of intimate family friend who could give guidance concerning words and actions to be used by those who were seeking to establish right relations with a higher power. Without pressing the parallel in detail, this was the general office of Jesus. He was still a member of the community of his brethren but, being also the Son of God, he could lead them into the enjoyment of an intimate communion with his Father-God. Thus as Son and as Paraclete he deals with our sins; it is in virtue of his sacrifice that he is able so to do; and by his living and eternal advocacy, he brings us near to God.

As we conclude this chapter, we would emphasize the fact that we have found no fully developed Atonement theory in the New Testament in terms of imagery drawn from the life of the home. We have sought only to gather together the significant metaphors which are employed and to show something of their suggestiveness for any later attempt to expound the doctrine more fully in this way.

6. The Cross in Christian Interpretation

"Christ crucified, unto the Jews a stumblingblock, and unto the Greeks foolishness; but unto them which are called, both Jews and Greeks, Christ the power of God, and the wisdom of God." —*I Cor. 1:23, 24.*

I

Before the last documents of the New Testament had been written, the Christian Church had become firmly established in the great cities of the Graeco-Roman world. Its ruling traditions were still those emanating from Palestine but it was being forced daily to come to terms with the new environment in which it was placed. By this time its language was mainly Greek and it was inevitable that its thought-forms and practices, as well as its language, should in some measure be influenced by the ancient civilization in which it lived. The process was almost imperceptibly slow but it was none the less sure; the great heritage of Old Testament and apostolic writings had gradually to be interpreted to new converts as they came into the Christian Church. How, for instance, could they be led to understand the meaning of the life and death and resurrection of Christ? What had they in their own background to which an appeal could be made? How could the normative verbs and names of the New Testament become dramatically significant to them and capable of moving them to sacrificial action and holiness of life? These questions were not easy to answer but they were insistent. Men and women were coming into the Christian Church without any background of the Old Testament revelation and it was no easy task to lead them to understand the significance of the death of the One whom they were taught to regard as divine.

At first, it would appear, little was done beyond taking the actual apostolic writings or symbols, and seeking to make their meaning clear to the hearers. This normally involved an attempt to portray out of common experience a situation in some way comparable to the dramatic event of Calvary. Certain well-defined patterns of behaviour are to be found amongst all peoples, and actions which fall within these patterns have meaning for the members of those societies to which they (the patterns) belong. Therefore, if an event or series of events from outside can in some way be compared to one of these patterns, it immediately takes on meaning for those who belong to that particular society. Thus, to take one example, the early Graeco-Roman society was familiar with the institution of slavery and with the particular action of ransoming a slave which came within the general pattern of that institution. When, therefore, the death of Christ was referred to as a ' ransom,' it immediately took on meaning for the whole body of people to whom the methods of dealing with slaves were well known. This way of interpreting the meaning of a complex of events we shall call the method of imaginative comparison and there can be little doubt that this was the method chiefly employed in the early Church. The verbs of the New Testament which we have studied lent themselves readily to this way of handling and thus, through word and sacrament, the Gospel facts of the death and resurrection of Christ became significant for large numbers of simple souls. As the Gospel became known in more sophisticated circles, however, other methods gradually came into use. Two in particular came to be employed through the course of the centuries and these we shall describe as deductive reasoning and inductive reasoning. We shall consider each in turn.

II

The method of deductive reasoning begins with the assumption that certain general principles concerning God and his relation to the universe may be taken for granted. It may be assumed, for instance, as amongst the Greek philosophers, that God is the Prime Mover of all things in the universe but that he is himself impassible; or it may be assumed that God is the Author of all that is good and beautiful and true and that he can have no contact with what is evil and ugly and false. Then on the basis of these assumptions and others like them, the attempt may be made to show that it was inherently necessary that Christ, assumed to be the Son of God, must die. To some extent this method was used by the early Christian thinkers of Alexandria, but in reality they were far more concerned about problems of being than about problems of action, and their chief contribution to the theology of the Church was in the realm of Christology. When it came to speaking of the death of Christ they were inclined to favour the method to which we have already referred; it was not until the eleventh century that a sustained effort was made to set forth the meaning of Christ's death by the deductive way. Possibly the most famous of such attempts in all Christian history is that of St. Anselm (1033–1109) and a brief glance at his book, *Cur Deus Homo,* will help to make clear how this method works out in practice.

Saint Anselm begins with certain fundamental assumptions. He feels that they are quite universal in their scope and that even pagans must be willing to admit their validity. First, it is clear to him that God exists and that he designed men for blessedness; over against this he sees disobedience and disorder in the universe and this is clearly contrary to the purpose of God; it cannot be, however, that what God had designed should be brought to nought and therefore some suitable means of restoration must be found. In order to determine what would constitute a fitting restoration, Anselm makes further assumptions about the nature of sin and its annulment. Thus he builds up a long and complicated chain of reasoning whereby he finally proves to the satisfaction of his interlocutor that Christ had to die in order that harmony might be restored to the universe and man might be saved. All is derived from certain general principles which he feels justified in assuming, and with their help he develops such a logical explanation of the death of Christ as will, he feels, make it meaningful to all who are willing to follow his argument carefully. The fatal defect in Anselm's method is, of course, that by no means all men are willing to grant him his assumptions, especially when it comes to the question of the nature of sin and its penalty. As we see now, Anselm's reasoning largely depended upon certain ideas of justice current in his day and although these would have been of great value as illustrations of universal principles, they could not serve as the final and absolute expressions of the principles themselves. The *Cur Deus Homo* still contains material of great interest and value but it cannot any longer be regarded as a completely logical exposition of the reason for, and consequently the meaning of, the death of Christ.

III

On the other side, the method of inductive reasoning begins with certain historical data. It regards as facts open to scientific investigation that Jesus lived and ministered in Galilee, that he came into conflict with the Jewish and Roman authorities and ultimately died upon the cross. It examines the narratives with great care and seeks to determine the causes which led men to behave as they did towards Jesus and the motives which lay behind his own reactions to the historical situation in which he found himself. Having constructed as accurate an account as possible of his life and passion and death, it proceeds to compare this with similar happenings in other historical situations and to draw up a series of general principles concerning human life and human behaviour which seem to explain why it was inevitable that Jesus should have suffered and died as he did. The world being the place that it is, Jesus being the kind of man that he was, no other outcome could have been expected than that he would be put to death as he actually was. In this way, the upholders of the inductive method judge that a perfectly satisfactory explanation has been given of the meaning of Jesus' death and though further scientific investigation may cause it to be modified in certain minor details, in general the problem may be regarded as solved.

As is well known the heyday for this particular method of approach was the latter half of the nineteenth century and the early years of the twentieth. In the early centuries of the Church's life the theologians of Antioch tended to rely upon the historical approach rather than upon the strictly philosophical but in no such thoroughgoing way as did the school of historical theology in the later period of which we have just spoken. At the time of the Reformation too there was a certain attempt to recover the actual history of the New Testament age but again with no such precision of method as characterized the investigators of the nineteenth century. For these latter found themselves provided with material and instruments unthought of by their predecessors. There were the manifold results of research by scientists in other fields — anthropology, archaeology, comparative religion and kindred sciences: there were dictionaries, learned articles and critical textual apparatus ready to their hands. With enthusiasm they set to work, endeavouring to dispose of problems which had never hitherto received a completely satisfactory solution.

One of the earliest problems calling for consideration was that of the method of the divine revelation to men: then there followed the question of the nature of the One who had always within Christian history been regarded as the unique agent of that revelation. Another question offering itself for renewed investigation was that of the meaning of the suffering and death of the historical Jesus. Throughout the history of the Christian Church, and especially since the time of the Reformation, this had been a matter of outstanding interest and the historians were keen to supply an answer which would dispose of the problem once and for all. In the case of so well-attested a fact as that of the death of Jesus, it surely should be possible to set out the causes and thereby determine a meaning which should be acceptable to all open-minded searchers after truth.

Possibly the most famous attempt of this kind was that made by the late Dean Rashdall in his Bampton Lectures of 1915. A brilliant historian, possessing a rich knowledge of ethical theories and judgements and ready to avail himself of the finest results of critical Biblical scholarship, seemed to be just the man to exploit the inductive method to the full. Yet in spite of the wealth of his learning and the high standard of his scientific investigations, the final result was, to say the least, disappointing. Jesus' death was to all intents and purposes a martyr's death: so great was his faithfulness and loyalty to God and his fellow men that nothing could turn him aside from the pathway of self-sacrifice, not even suffering and death; and when these were inflicted upon him, the fine quality of his spirit shone out and his patience and forgivingness remained as a permanent legacy to all mankind.[1]

Two of the fatal defects of this method can readily be seen. In the first place, although the investigator attempts to make an absolutely unbiased approach, laying aside all preconceptions and examining the evidence with fair and balanced judgement, in reality he is never able to eliminate the personal equation entirely.[2] Thus in the case of Dr. Rashdall there is no doubt where his own sympathies lay, and when it came to examining certain texts of the New Testament he allowed himself to deal with them in a way which was arbitrary in the extreme. The fact is that when it comes to estimating the significance of a particular group of historical events, a man cannot avoid appealing to his own experience of life and allowing thereby a certain subjectivity to enter into his final judgement. In the second place, although the investigator seeks to gather together all the available material before setting out general principles or framing definite results, there is always the possibility that he may have overlooked some piece of evidence which is of vital importance for the matter in hand. Especially when the subject for consideration is the meaning of a historical incident, some relatively tiny factor, some indication, for example, of the state of mind of the chief actor, may have an exceedingly weighty contribution to make towards the final result. Thus both because of the personal predilections of the investigator and because of the impossibility of gathering together the whole body of evidence necessary for a final judgement, the inductive method can never give a final and absolutely authoritative answer to any problem of historical meaning. Above all is this the case when the matter for consideration desiderates a meaning which is not merely on the human level but in some way includes the divine. No purely human investigation can include all the divine possibilities. While recognizing therefore the value and indeed the necessity of as careful and thorough a scientific examination of the historical data as can be made, our final conclusion must be that this, of itself, will not be sufficient to provide us with the meaning which we seek.

IV

Having failed to discover a fully satisfactory method in either of those which we have considered, we turn back to the first method — that of imaginative comparison. In this approach we do not reject either the deductive or the inductive entirely. In accordance with the former method, we make the fundamental assumption that man was created in the image of God and that the relationships between God and his creatures may therefore be spoken of in terms taken from the personal intercourse between man and man: this does not mean that the relationships are fully comprehended within these terms but it does mean that these terms are able to give a rough sketch, a preliminary imaginative portrayal of those relationships, in a way which is in some measure true to the reality represented. Further we assume that the central witness of the New Testament concerning the death of Christ may be used as an outline for the development of fuller meaning. If this assumption cannot be granted, then we are cut off from historic Christianity altogether. If the early Christians were entirely wrong when they claimed that Christ died for their sins according to the Scriptures, then the apostles started off on a completely false trail and we have no means of ascertaining the true meaning of the mission of Christ at all. Without the assumption that the original relationship between God and men had somehow been broken by man's unfaithfulness and that restoration had been made by the historic life of Jesus Christ culminating in his cross and resurrection, we cannot make any sense of early Christianity, and the New Testament becomes a dangerously misleading and ultimately worthless book. If, then, we are to have any hope of discovering a meaning which is more than a mere outworking of a succession of natural causes, we are surely justified in starting with the assumptions which we have just outlined to see if they lead us to any meaningful conclusions in terms of present-day thought.

These assumptions to which we have just referred may be set out more clearly as follows. We hold that there is a living God who created man in his own image, desiring that he should dwell in a perfect personal relationship with himself: thus in the original pattern of human life, relationships between man and man bore a clear resemblance to relationships between man and God. We hold, further, that through the sin of mankind this relationship was spoiled and broken, though the original pattern of human life was not entirely destroyed: relationships between man and man still carry traces of the perfect relationships which should exist between man and God (otherwise the parables of Jesus become unintelligible). Finally we hold that through the life, death and resurrection of Jesus Christ, and particularly through his death, because it was there that the whole process came to its focus, the relationship was restored and the way opened for man to live anew according to God's original design.

It may be said at once that these are tremendous assumptions and there can be no doubt that they are. At the same time, it must be urged that they are the basic assumptions (or beliefs) of historic Christianity from its very inception, and if they are false, any enquiry about the meaning of Christ's work is hardly worth making. Moreover, no attempt is made to claim that they are more than assumptions. We have presented them in the barest possible form. We begin with them as postulates or axioms and seek to ask whether they can be clothed with life and meaning by the aid of material drawn from history and our experience of life today. If this cannot be done, then we may certainly abandon them, for they evidently have no value for our own day and generation. If, however, we find that they begin to illuminate the whole of hu-

man existence, if they shed light upon the significance of the
whole course of human history, then surely our assumptions
will not have been wholly unjustified — at least they have a
right to stand until such time as other thinkers, starting with
other presuppositions, are able to give a more meaningful answer to the problems of human life.

We do not then altogether reject the method of deductive
reasoning; nor, in the second place, do we altogether reject that
of inductive reasoning. We have just spoken of the necessity of
clothing our assumed framework with life and meaning by the
aid of material drawn from history and our experience of life
today. In doing this we are bound to pay as careful attention
as possible to all that historical research can teach us: (1)
about mankind in general; (2) about those who have lived in
specially intimate relationship with God; and (3), and above
all, about Him whose life and death form the subject of our
ultimate enquiry. Combining with this rich store of material
which history provides the insights into the nature of basic
human relationships which men of wide experience and sound
learning can give, we shall seek to make imaginative comparisons between dramatic events such as might happen upon
the human plane and the supreme dramatic event which took
place, as we believe, within the economy of God. By such comparisons, that event will become meaningful as in no other
way, and although we shall never come near to exhausting
its meaning, we shall perhaps succeed in making that meaning more vivid to our own minds and to those of our fellows
within the contemporary scene.

V

In adopting this method of imaginative comparison we are
not, of course, venturing upon a new and untrodden path.

This was the method of the Old Testament prophets as they employed word pictures and symbolic gestures to portray God's relationships with men; it was the method of our Lord himself and later of his apostles. They did not build up logical arguments, nor did they engage in scientific analysis; rather, they used vivid words and metaphors drawn from human life and used them to bring home to men's minds the significance of the Gospel which they proclaimed. Likewise, in the succeeding centuries of the Church's history, it was the men who used striking comparisons and richly imaginative language who were able to impress their readers or hearers and make a permanent contribution to thought on the Atonement. Irenaeus and Origen with their pictures of the conflict with the Devil, Tertullian and Anselm with their metaphors taken from legal processes, Luther and Aulén with their military comparisons, McLeod Campbell and Moberly with their vivid illustrations taken from the life of the home — these constitute the great names in Atonement doctrine, not so much on account of their power of deductive reasoning but rather because of their fertile imaginations and power of metaphorical expression. And today there is a growing recognition that abstract generalizations, valuable as they may be in their own way, are little able to move the mind and will of man.

Consider, for example, the words of two recent Gifford Lecturers, men who are amongst the leading thinkers of our day. " If I were asked," writes Professor Macneile Dixon, " what has been the most powerful force in the making of history, you would probably judge me of unbalanced mind were I to answer, as I should have to answer, metaphor, figurative expression. It is by imagination that men have lived; imagination rules all our lives. The human mind is not, as philosophers would have you think, a debating hall but a picture gallery." [3] In similar vein, Professor Kroner speaks of imagination as " the architect of our future world, the intrinsic motor of our private and public life." In a notable discussion of the religious function of imagination, he claims that religion more than philosophy, and certainly more than science, is able to penetrate to the heart of things. The deepest questions in life are those concerning God and man and here the imagination is far superior to logical and scientific thought. It creates images and links them together, and " our inner life is determined by images, produced by practical imagination. For our real life is not intellectual only; it is the life of our heart and our will as well. And the language of our heart and our will is the language of imagination, as every preacher and every orator knows." [4]

Or take the words of an expert in literary studies. Professor F. C. Prescott, of Cornell, has an interesting and illuminating book dealing with the operation of the poet's mind. In this he considers at length the nature and function of the imagination in man, and we may draw upon some of his conclusions. Early in the book he makes a fundamental distinction between two modes of thought. There is, on the one hand, the imaginative, sensuous, concrete; on the other hand, the purposive, analytical, abstract. The first is pre-eminently the mode employed by children and primitive folk; the second comes more and more into prominence in adult life and in civilizations which have become highly developed and organized. But Professor Prescott will not allow that the second way is necessarily superior to the first. " Because we speak of the imaginative way of thinking as primitive," he says, " we are tempted to think of it as inferior. And indeed there are other reasons why we should depreciate it. Our growth in command of voluntary thought, in power of reasoning, has been so remarkable, we have come to depend on reasoning so exclusively and the products of our reasoning in modern science have been of such immediate and immense practical value, that we are inclined to undervalue the other faculty; the younger brother looks down upon the elder. But the other faculty is still as valuable as ever. The heart still sees further than the head. . . . If we look at it broadly enough we shall see that the older faculty in many respects is still the better." [5]

From this the author goes on to urge the vital necessity of recapturing, as far as we can, the power of imaginative thought. Especially should this be the case in relation to subjects which are beyond our comprehension. Wherever there is, what one writer has called " an apperceptive insufficience," *there* is the precise field for the imagination to have its fullest sway. So we may well infer that in approaching such a subject as the coming together of God and man in and through the Atonement wrought by Christ, man cannot simply reason in logical terms; he can only imagine and believe. [6] Taking images gained through his experience of life, he can employ them in various ways to suggest the great reality of which we have just spoken; more than this he cannot do. As Professor Prescott says later in his book, " All human thought proceeds ultimately through a recognition of relations and likenesses." [7] To see and feel resemblances between typical happenings in human life and the great act accomplished by Christ upon the cross — this is the all-important task of those who would seek to bring home the significance of Calvary to the men and women of their day.

VI

This decision to employ the language of the imagination rather than of scientific logic may seem to many so open to criticism that a further attempt to justify our method must be made. Let us first, then, ask what is the exact function of scientific logic. It is, we believe, in the last resort to deal with objects and events belonging to the impersonal universe in which we live. In some mysterious way, the mind of man is *en rapport* with this universe and is able to represent objects and events within it by words. As, then, all objects within the universe are linked together by intricate connections making up one harmonious whole (this, at least, we assume) , so the mind of man seeks to apprehend these objects and events by words and to connect his words in ways corresponding to the connections of the universe outside. All the time he must check his thinking against the objective facts, though he is always at liberty to make hypotheses and to seek to verify them through further investigation. What constitutes logical thinking is the establishment of as close a correspondence as possible between the words which man uses and the objects and events which they describe. Thus all impersonal phenomena, even man when regarded purely from the point of view of his position as an objective entity within the universe, form the subject matter for scientific logic. Deductively, assumptions can be made and results worked out and checked by experiment; inductively, observations may be made and results worked out and general laws obtained. Thus the two methods work hand in hand in helping to establish an ever closer correspondence between the objective reality of the universe and the representation of that reality supplied by the words of the human mind.

When, however, we come to consider the actions of men as *persons,* we find ourselves in a different situation. No longer is there simply a correspondence between the external object and the thinking mind; now there are communications between persons, and the question arises as to how these communications are made. All experience goes to show that they are not made simply *in vacuo.* There must be a common medium, but where, we ask, is this to be found? The answer surely must be that it is the impersonal universe which forms the medium, though now man confronts it not simply with the purpose of establishing a direct correspondence between its objects or events and his own mind, but rather with the desire to find in them a symbol or metaphor to represent the particular communication which he desires to make to his fellow man. Thus two persons may each have a scientific relation to the universe and each will express it in much the same way; but in relations with one another, since they are mutually dependent upon symbols, relations, likenesses, it is impossible for them to express the ultimate mystery of their personal relationship within strictly scientific and logical terms.

Now it is our ultimate faith that God has created man to exist ever in a dual relationship. On the one hand he is related to the impersonal universe in a way which we may call direct correspondence; on the other hand, he is related to the world of persons in a way which we may call indirect communication. For his thinking in relation to the former, he will use the ordinary words of direct representation, but in relation to the latter he must use words of imaginative comparison, though these will never be altogether independent of the impersonal universe from which they were originally derived.

Coming, then, to the relations between God and man: if God were impersonal, if he were simply part of the impersonal universe, acting therein only in impersonal ways, then the language of scientific logic would be sufficient for every description of the relations between God and man. If, however, God is personal and enters into personal relations with men, then scientific logic alone is not sufficient. We must turn to the metaphor and the image and the symbol if the communication is to have any meaning to us at all. In other words, the language of personal communication must be used in speaking of any personal approach of God to man.

Now God's word to man through the cross (if indeed it was

such) is no exception to this rule. The complex of events there enacted partook to some extent of the nature of impersonal observable phenomena: to that extent they can be represented by scientific terms within the human mind and these can be checked by all the tests which the science of history supplies. But in so far as that complex of events partook of the nature of the *personal* and expressed a word of personal communication from God to man, no scientific logic can finally represent it. Only by means of imaginative comparison, only by visualizing, within the general pattern of human life, situations and events comparable to that supreme event, can we respond to it meaningfully and interpret it in its character as the very Word and Revelation of God to man.

VII

Having thus decided upon the general method which we shall employ in seeking to draw out the meaning of the death of Christ, we shall conclude this chapter by indicating what are the sources from which we shall draw our images and comparisons. A good deal of work hitherto has suffered, in our judgement, from the tendency of writers or preachers to ' mix metaphors.' Words or phrases are used which apply primarily to one area of life and are freely combined with others which belong to a different area. Thus a writer may give an exposition couched mainly in legal terms. Obviously he is drawing parallels in his mind between the subject under review and the outworking of communal justice. But then suddenly, and generally unconsciously, he will introduce other metaphors, taken perhaps from family life, and will confuse the issue by leading the reader to infer that motives and processes belonging to the one area are perfectly in place in the other. This, however, is simply not true. There cannot indeed be a rigid division of human existence into watertight compartments, but at the same time actions which are normal and natural within the home would be totally out of place in the courts of public justice. It follows, then, that words and metaphors drawn from family life can only be used with the greatest care in an entirely different context, and all in all it will make for clarity if we try first to define our imaginative fields and then endeavour to move, now within one, now within another, as we proceed to make our comparisons.

Our fundamental claim is that there are four great areas of the imagination from which words and metaphors may be drawn. These areas cover the whole of human existence and it is probable that every man has at least some experience within each. The precise structure of these areas will differ from generation to generation and from people to people, but not entirely so. Always, we believe, it will be possible to discover some common pattern, some comparable elements, and therefore a meaningful exposition derived from any one of these fields will contain something of universal relevance. These areas we shall now briefly describe.

The first corresponds to the struggle of life, that struggle in which all mankind is, in some form, engaged: the struggle with the elements, the struggle with the earth, the struggle with pestilence and disease, the struggle with other members of society, the struggle with demonic powers. The second corresponds to the ordering of the life of the community: the establishment of law, the administration of justice, co-operation and collaboration for the common good, the maintenance of harmony and peace. The third corresponds to the creative activity of men: the construction of useful and beautiful objects, the development of the arts, the advancement of science, the upbuilding of all that is included within the general term 'culture' within the life of mankind. The fourth and last corresponds to the life of the family: the provision of a centre of shelter and protection, the nurture of the young, the warmth of mutual love, the experience of the most intimate personal relationship. Within these four areas — the field of conflict, the life of community, the development of culture, the intimacy of the home — the whole of human existence is encompassed. We propose now to take up a temporary residence within each of these fields and to draw upon the resources which each provides for amplifying and enriching the bare sketch which we earlier set before our minds of the severing and restoring of the relationship between God and man.[8]

7. The Cross as Redemptive Conflict

"For even the Son of man came not to be ministered unto, but to minister, and to give his life a ransom for many."
— Mark 10:45.

In entering life," wrote Voltaire, " we enter war." Few would be prepared to deny the essential truth of this challenging claim. In the midst of a world war it becomes more than ever clear that life is a mighty struggle, but even in times of so-called peace the element of conflict is never absent from the basic pattern of human existence. Man does not glide smoothly through his earthly span of existence but finds himself involved in tensions and testings from beginning to end. He is by no means " a detached thinker, surveying the universe from a secure vantage point, but a creature exposed to the play of mighty forces and inextricably involved in increasing conflict." [1] Often this conflict is brought about by pressures within his economic life; since prehistoric days, says Max Huber, the great international jurist, in the Oxford Conference Report, " the tension between the needs of a people and the space it occupies has been the impelling force in the history of mankind. Where this tension has not been relieved by labour, that is by the extensive exploitation of one's own soil or by the enjoyment of the advantages of space in another country . . . this produces violent outbreaks." Or again, the tension may be produced by the growth of industrialization and a consequent rivalry between the urban and rural communities; it may be produced by an influx of new ideas which threaten to undermine the foundations of existing society. However the tension may be caused, it remains a fact that man is always struggling to live, struggling either with the soil, or

113

with new conditions of life, or with the forces which control production and distribution, or with his fellow men, or with himself.

The fact of man's life being essentially a conflict has been eloquently expressed in what I regard as two of the great books of modern times. One is Mr. Arnold Toynbee's *Study of History,* the thesis of which is that all human progress and development follow the pattern of what he calls challenge and response. He writes of the stimulus of hard countries, of new ground, of blows, of pressures, of penalizations, and of the reactions of different peoples at different periods of the world's history and of the effects upon their growth and development. It is a fascinating study, and one comes away from it, at least, with the feeling that nothing worth-while is won in life without a struggle. Similarly there are Professor Macneile Dixon's Gifford Lectures which he entitles *The Human Situation.* The burden of his message to this generation is that the indispensable ingredient in a recipe for a true life is conflict and struggle. He quotes Blake: " Without contraries is no progression "; he quotes Hegel: " Nothing great in the world is accomplished without passion "; he appeals to what is at the heart of the teaching of modern science: " that in the absence of resistance, energy has no power and vanishes." And in one of the most thrilling passages of the book, where he compares life to the sea, he concludes by recalling the incident of Leonidas at Thermopylae, who, while resolved himself to stand and die for his country's cause, wished to save two lads by sending them home with a message to Sparta. He was met by the answer, " We are not here to carry messages, but to fight."

I

Life, then, is a conflict,[2] and in the struggle the central figure has ever been the leader, the pioneer, the hero, the

archēgos, as the writer of The Epistle to the Hebrews so vividly calls him. And the Bible does not hesitate to use this
imagery in describing God's relation to his people: he is their
Leader and Champion, and they are ideally his loyal and faithful followers.[3] But now the question arises. How are we to
analyze the relationship between the Champion and his followers? What description of it will capture the imagination
of our fellows? Surely there is little question that the relationship must be interpreted in a double way. On the one side
there is demand, on the other side gift; on the one side requirement, on the other side promise. What, for instance, do
we find the leaders of the world calling for from their followers in these days? We find the call to uncompromising devotion, to an undivided loyalty, to a complete self-sacrifice, to
an unswerving allegiance. We find no hesitation on the part
of the leader to summon his followers to hardship and suffering and even death itself. We need only refer to the speeches
of Mr. Winston Churchill after Dunkirk to find this constantly recurring note — the call for resolute and devoted
service, for the expenditure of blood and sweat and tears, for
the outpouring of life to the uttermost because of the struggle
in which men were engaged. Men are prepared to be challenged absolutely by a man who is really worthy of the name
leader.

Yet it is clear that the relation of the leader to his followers
is not simply that of call and demand: there is always promise
too. And we believe that if the nature of this promise is closely
examined it will be found always to imply some new freedom
for those who are willing to engage in the strife. Freedom is
a magic word and one which has nerved men for conflict and
struggle in a way which none other has been able to do.

Before proceeding further, however, let us try to understand more fully what this promise of freedom really contains.
What do we mean by freedom? What does freedom connote in
our modern world? It is all very well to wax rhetorical as a

famous United States Senator did not long ago in Halifax and say that " we shall bring freedom to the race of man, we shall strike down tyranny, uproot force, chain the gods of war tighter than ever Prometheus was bound," but what does it all mean positively? It is all very well to shout on St. George's Day that Britons never, never, never shall be slaves, but what is to save such shouting from being the merest claptrap? What positive conception of liberty can we place before men?

No recent pronouncement has, I suppose, met with so marked a response as has that of President Roosevelt, made at the beginning of 1941. Freedom, he said, must involve four elements. There must be freedom from want and from fear, coupled with freedom of speech and freedom of worship. Such a definition is certainly valuable as far as it goes, but it may be doubted if it goes far enough.

There is too much of the suggestion that men dwelling in safety on a well-stocked island, at liberty to say anything they pleased and to worship anything they wished, would be truly free. Yet this would be only a travesty of freedom. The only one of the four which seems to us to draw near to the heart of things is freedom of worship. For worship holds within it the thought of valuation, and surely it is in pursuit of a valued interest, in bending all energies towards the attainment of a particular goal, that true freedom is discovered and enjoyed. As Professor Perry, of Harvard, points out in his book *Shall Not Perish from the Earth,* liberty can exist only *in relation* to some interest or desire (or we may say value) on the part of mankind. When there is a positive and a worth-while goal, then man can begin to talk about freedom, for it consists negatively in the removal of obstacles to the attainment of the goal and positively in the bestowal of power to speed him on his way thereto. But the important thing is that liberty or freedom is utterly meaningless apart from its relation to an interest or value or goal.

One further thing, however, remains to be said. In promising men freedom, the leader has in his own mind the goal which is to be the object of the quest. It is not for the follower to define the goal; if he desires the freedom which the leader promises, he must be prepared to accept the proposed objective as worthy of his wholehearted endeavour. Thus we may sum up our first analysis by saying that the leader calls men to follow him in the pursuit of a certain value or goal; that he demands from them an absolute loyalty and devoted allegiance; and that at the same time he offers them release from all the disabilities which would hinder them, together with power sufficient to meet every emergency on the way. Paradoxically, it is in his service that men are to find their perfect freedom.

II

All the great epics of the world, I suppose, illustrate the general thesis that I have just set out. Almost every people loves to recount the stories of its heroes of past days — men who are often idealized and in many cases raised to the rank of divinity — men who exercised an extraordinary influence in their own generation, calling out unqualified devotion and inspiring to feats of amazing courage and endurance. One and all these heroes and leaders made their demands, gave their promises, and men responded. But this is not all the story. Again and again history records how men have been unfaithful to their leaders, have rejected their demands and spurned their promises, have mutinied, apostatized, have given up the struggle. The challenge has seemed too great, the reward too small, the demand too costly, the promise too shadowy, and so men have grown weary, lost hope, abandoned the struggle, turned back, gone home. These are the tragedies and follies of history, the inglorious episodes in the life of mankind.

No more vivid example of this whole process could be found than that which is provided by the historical narrative of the Old Testament. Essentially, God was the Leader of his people. He set before them a goal, summoned them to his allegiance, broke down the Egyptian bondage, and saved them through the waters of the Red Sea. At Sinai he issued the call to a new loyalty and bound them to himself by a solemn covenant: as the living, jealous God, he could brook no divided allegiance. Then, further, he led them through the wilderness and brought them to the Land of Promise. The whole story is couched in terms of a divine Commander with his band of followers — calling out their loyalty, providing for their needs, inspiring them with courage and hope. In all their affliction he was afflicted, and not an angel, not an earthly messenger, but his own Presence saved them. This is without doubt the dominating field of imagination in the historical books of the Old Testament.

But within this same context, there is another picture which constantly recurs. It is the picture of an unfaithful, apostate people, departing from the living God. That is the root conception of sin in the Old Testament: it is apostasy, disloyalty, treachery, mutiny. Israel turns aside, becomes unfaithful, goes after other leaders, human or divine; she tries to divide her allegiance, she hankers after an easier life, she chafes at the hardships which her following of Yahweh entails. Moreover, she ceases to look for the coming of the promise: instead she looks back longingly to the fleshpots of Egypt and yearns to exchange the shadow of the future for the substance of the past. That is sin — the root of sin in the Old Testament — on the one hand, disloyalty in rejecting God's demands; on the other hand, apostasy in despising his promises.

Now the record of the Old Testament might be described as one of ever-deepening gloom. The idyllic days were the wilderness days when in a more vivid way than at any other period of the national history God was the leader. But even in wilderness days, as some of those great dramatic poems of the psalter show, there was apostasy and unfaithfulness; yet this was as little compared with the apostasy of Jeroboam, the son of Nebat, who made Israel to sin, or the sheer paganism of Manasseh, king of Judah, who brought disaster upon his people. Finally there came the Exile and black despair. The results of sin were now clearly revealed. On the one hand, to turn away from loyalty to God was to become enslaved by some earthly demonry; on the other hand, to despise God's promise and the hope which it gives was to surrender oneself to hopelessness and despair.

This old story is of the greatest help to us as we seek to gain a more general view of the relationship between God and man in terms of images drawn from the field of human conflict and struggle. As I have suggested, we think of God setting before men a goal of life: calling them to loyalty and devotion to himself in the pursuit of that goal, and at the same time promising them true freedom as they press onwards in their quest in dependence upon him. But men have despised the divine goal of life and set their hearts on objectives which are temporal and ephemeral: they have given their allegiance to other leaders — human and demonic; they have rejected the promises of God and sought liberty in the pursuit of their own earth-bound goals. The result has been a growing attachment to demonic powers and thereby a progressive enslavement to the enemies of God, coupled with a growing disillusionment and hopelessness leading to the frenzy of despair.

III

Let me, if I may, comment on each of these a little more fully in the light of our present situation. Think first of the aspect of *enslavement*. Is it not enforced submission to some temporal institution or power which has no eternal sanction: a Church, a State, a social system, a dictator, an economic régime? If these are not related to God but are simply self-contained entities, they are only of time and have no eternal reference: to yield oneself, body and soul, to such is to become enslaved to something which must ultimately pass away. Or from another angle, what is slavery but attachment to some fixed entity which is really dead: a dogma or a law, a theory or a custom? If these are not vitally related to God, they are moribund, and to be bound to one of them is to be attached to a putrefying corpse.

But is not that the state of our world today? In its repudiation of God it has become enslaved to ' isms ' and ' olatries.' Like Samson, having turned away from the living God, our generation stands, in the words of one of our leading novelists, " eyeless in Gaza," and seems to be straining to pull down about its ears this scientific civilization which has won its allegiance.

> " But what more oft in nations grown corrupt,
> And by their vices brought to servitude,
> Than to love bondage more than liberty —
> Bondage with ease than strenuous liberty —
> And to despise, or envy, or suspect
> Whom God hath of his special favor raised
> As their deliverer? " [4]

Or think of the aspect of *hopelessness*. Is not this a characteristic of our world? There is little doubt that the frenzied

despair of Germany today is the direct outcome of the hopelessness which had settled down upon that country like a
thick pall some fourteen or fifteen years ago. Likewise there
is little doubt that the more apathetic hopelessness which at
least till recently possessed the soul of France was the direct
outcome of the utter disillusionment which succeeded upon
the hollow victory of 1918. While men's hearts are set upon
the establishment of some merely earthly security, living only
for the present and indifferent to the future, hopelessness is
bound to ensue. And in those impressive words from *The
Keys of the Kingdom,* " Hell is the place where one has ceased
to hope."

This, then, is the state of the human race as envisaged
within this imaginative field. It is enslaved to earthly principalities and powers, fulfilling meaningless, habitual, mechani-
cal actions which have no eternal significance; it is also living
under the domination of present possessions with no hope and
little desire for the future. It is an age which talks constantly
of freedom and has little conception of what freedom really
is; it is an age which is much concerned about the new order
but is confused as to what it means and has grave doubts
whether it will ever come into being. But in all this our own
age is not unique: it could probably have been written
equally well of the Hellenistic age of the first century or the
Rationalist age of the eighteenth century. It is true of mankind in every age inasmuch as mankind in its sin has been
unfaithful to God its Saviour and Redeemer.[5]

IV

Is that, then, all that can be said? Is God content that his
victory shall tarry forever and the powers of darkness remain
masters of this world of men? The whole message of the Chris-

tian Gospel is that such is not the case. God sets his people
free and redeems them to himself in and through Jesus Christ.
A radical change is made in the entire situation, and this is
what, within this field of the imagination, is meant by the
Atonement.

How, then, are we to interpret this as taking place? Let us
ask first how within the sphere of human history the great
deliverances have been effected. They have in almost every
case, I think, been due to a champion or saviour. For his task
he has two essential qualifications:

1. He identifies himself absolutely with the enslaved people whom he is seeking to serve. He shares their manner of
life, their hardship and bitterness, allows the iron of their
circumstances to enter into his soul. He knows their estate
intimately and, like the king of the Old Testament in the time
of famine and siege, wears sackcloth within upon his flesh.

2. At the same time he brings with him an inner vision and
a power all his own. Though sharing the circumstances, he
has no intention of being bound by the circumstances; though
engulfed in an atmosphere of hopelessness, he never ceases to
hope. In fact, even in the midst of abject bondage, he already
lives a life of freedom which he is determined shall be the
possession also of those whom he seeks to deliver.

The leader then is a man of vision, power, and inner freedom, who voluntarily surrenders all personal privilege and
identifies himself in all outward conditions with the people
who are enslaved. Then, when the time is ripe, when his
identification is sufficiently complete and his own manifestation of true liberty sufficiently disclosed, he challenges the
tyrannical powers to mortal combat and, if successful in the
fight, leads out his followers into freedom from bondage and
newness of life. Many examples could be given of this process
from the distant past down to the present day. No more noble
illustration from among humankind could be found than that

of Moses, a man who had gained strength and vision and inner
freedom in the Mount and who proceeded therefrom to a
period of absolute identification with the Children of Israel
in the bondage of Egypt. At the decisive moment he challenged the enslaving powers and led the people out from
darkness to light and from bondage to liberty, a liberty more
essentially spiritual and ethical than any other that has been
achieved for men save that of Jesus Christ himself. Or, to
take an example from our own day, what is more striking in
the life of Toyohiko Kagawa than the way in which he learned
what it meant to be really identified with the lowest of his
own people? Few stories make a deeper impression on modern youth than that of this young Japanese who at the age of
twenty-one, while still a college student, suddenly plunged
into the depths of the Shinkawa slums. There in a wretched
hut he lived and witnessed, never refusing to share his bed
and bedding with the most degraded and diseased. He himself
contracted infectious ailments and a disease of the eyes, but
he never flinched. In the words of his biographer:

" Kagawa put the drive of a great heart into the work
of picking brands out of the fire. He conquered through
love, but it was no easy victory. Love's victories are never
cheaply won. They are secured at a fearful price. Christ
conquered only through the Cross. His envoy in Shinkawa looked upon privations, insults, and attacks as mere
incidents of the day's work. Others looked upon these
people as alley spawn, a breed of the underworld. He
looked upon them as folk. He loved them. He saw hidden
in each one a priceless soul and a potential personality." [6]

But Kagawa was not satisfied simply to be identified with
these people in their squalor. He looked for the day when he
could lead them out into a new freedom. Many of them were
slowly coming to a consciousness of their latent worth and
were only waiting for a leader who could organize their forces
and champion their cause.

" Kagawa was the man for the hour. He had lived with them. He had suffered with them. He had wept with them. He knew them better than they knew themselves. Their cause was his cause. Their battle was his battle." [7]

And, we may add, his aim was ever to make his victory their victory.

V

If now we agree to accept these two principles as valid within the sphere of the human conflict, we shall not, I think, find difficulty in applying them to the thought of the deliverance which has been wrought by Christ Jesus our Lord. First of all, we need not dwell overmuch on the fact of his complete identification with enslaved and hopeless humanity. If there is one theme which the New Testament emphasizes again and again it is surely this: " The Word became flesh and made his dwelling among us." " Ye know the grace of our Lord Jesus Christ, that, though he was rich, yet for your sakes he became poor." " He who was in the form of God thought it not a thing to be grasped after to be on an equality with God, but emptied himself." What the theologians of the last half century have been trying to express by their theories of Kenosis is simply this essential concept that the Son of God fully and completely identified himself with the human race which he came to save, *apart from sin*. Tested in all points like as we are, sharing human limitations, experiencing to the full the heat and passion of the human conflict, he was man among men, able to operate from within the very citadel of enslaved humanity and so to be, in an absolute and final sense, men's Champion and Redeemer.

We turn then to the other side which is not quite so obvious but which surely needs equal emphasis. He was him-

self without sin: that is, within the imaginative field which
we are at present considering, he was guiltless of those attitudes which mankind as a whole has taken up in relation to
God their Leader and Saviour. Disloyalty and apostasy, such
as we considered earlier in the chapter, were to him unknown;
contempt of God's blessings and promises were to him un-
thinkable. So we see in his words and in his life a manifestation of utter loyalty to God on the one hand and an unswerving trust in his promises on the other. He passed through this
earthly scene, sharing all its limitations and conflicts, but
without a shadow of disloyalty to God who was his leader.
He was God's Servant (as we saw earlier, the word is taken
from The Book of Isaiah and was clearly accepted by our
Lord at his baptism), and as such would be loyal even to the
death. No matter how subtly the powers of darkness might
seek to deflect his loyalty even by a hairsbreadth, he refused
to yield, and emerged from his temptations strong as tem-
pered steel. Similarly he never once staggered at the promises
of God. The Kingdom of his God, the new order of righteousness and peace and joy in the Holy Ghost, the sphere of true
liberty and life, was a hope of which he was never ashamed.
His confidence that that Kingdom must be established never
faltered, and in an amazing way he lived already as a member of that Kingdom, enjoying its liberty, even while still a
sojourner on earth. He passed through this earthly life as One
who already reigned just because he was already conscious of
the royal freedom of heaven.

Then at last the time came for him to throw down the gage
to the principalities and powers which bound men in chains.
All human institutions which were claiming an *absolute* loyalty from men, he deliberately opposed and challenged. The
Pharisees, custodians of the religious system; the Temple authorities, custodians of the economic system; the chief priests
and scribes, custodians of the political system — he chal-

lenged them all to mortal combat and at the same time openly
set at nought those values of earth which had been erected in
place of the values of the Kingdom of God. Men had grasped
the substance of earth in place of what they regarded as the
shadow of heaven; he grasped the substance of heaven in place
of what he regarded as the shadow of earth. On the battlefield
of Calvary he engaged the tyrannous powers which enslaved
men; he went into battle trusting in the promises of God, re-
joicing in the joy that was set before him, and despising the
cross with all its shame. Of that supreme conflict we dare not
speak lightly: at times the issue seemed to hang in the very
balance, for agelong traditions, institutions, principalities,
powers were not to be easily overcome. In fact, as night fell
and man's last enemy, death, stood guard over his lifeless
body, it seemed that the battle had been lost. But our Christ
goes marching on! " Christus Victor " is the Church's confession. That Leader and Hero, who in life had been gloriously free from earth's bondage and despair, could not be
bound even in death. So he cut away the angelic rulers and
powers from us, exposing them to all the world and triumph-
ing over them in the cross. " O death, where is thy sting? O
grave, where is thy victory? . . . Thanks be to God, which
giveth us the victory through our Lord Jesus Christ."

VI

Thus atonement has been made; the victory has been won;
freedom has been secured. All that remains is for men to identify themselves with their Captain in his great deliverance
and march out into liberty and life. For, as Dr. Forsyth says,
God's redemption in Christ " is not simply an act of manifestation or even impressive manifestation . . . but it is a
historical and eternal act of deliverance prolonged in an in-

finite number of acts of the same kind in the experience of Christian people of their redemption 'in Christ.' " [8]

For St. Paul, this redemption could only be realized in actual experience through an identification with Christ so complete as almost to beggar description: in fact, his only way of speaking of it is in terms of crucifixion and death and resurrection parallel to Christ's own. " I have been crucified with Christ," he cries. " The world is crucified unto me, and I unto the world." Yet such language is not to be taken lightly. " To pass from the fundamental spirit of the world to the spirit of Christ," writes Dr. Herbert H. Farmer, " is not a matter of easy growth, gentle transition, natural evolution. It is not a matter of polite and mutual tolerance, and agreement to differ, as gentlemen should, on one or two more or less important points. It is an uprooting, rending, tearing, splitting and breaking, surgical-operation kind of thing, a mutual crucifixion, with nails and spears and agony and death." [9] This is a hard saying, but it reveals the only way of true freedom. For having identified himself with Christ in his crucifixion with all the cost involved, St. Paul found himself released from the bondage of sin and self and the world, living a new life of liberty wherein it was no longer he who lived but Christ who lived in him. The Spirit of the living Christ had set him free, and his life henceforth was one of faith in the Son of God, who had loved him and given himself up for him.

It was in the strength of this Spirit that he could now go forth to his life of labour and witness in which, having once for all been set free from the world, he was able to identify himself afresh with the world and participate in Christ's work of redemption of men. Never, surely, has there been such a case of complete identification with all sorts and conditions of men as was seen in the life of St. Paul. To the Jews he became as a Jew; to those without the law, as himself without law; to the weak, he became weak; he became all things to all men that by all means he might save some. This is the Spirit which has inspired all true missionaries ever since. Speaking of them in a striking passage, Dr. Forsyth exclaims: " How the missionaries do lose themselves to the people! Traders go to make fortunes and return home to enjoy them. But missionaries grow into their people." It is by such an identification alone, by a veritable ' growth into their people,' that Christ's followers can become united with him in his saving and redeeming work.

But not only is the redeeming process reproduced in individual lives; it manifests itself also in the life of the Church as a whole. Thus the central theme of the book of The Revelation of John is that the holy community, the Church, stands over against the demonic empire, the tyranny of Rome.[10] She is commissioned to fight out on earth the great supramundane conflict between God and Satan; but because the Lamb has won the victory, her ultimate triumph is also sure. Yet the conflict is intense, the suffering severe; the Church is a martyr Church and is called to be faithful unto death. She becomes in very truth a partaker in the blood of the Lamb by sharing in his tribulation and suffering. At the same time she shares in the supreme joy of his victory and overcomes through her stedfast witness to him.

Such a picture of suffering and victory within the community is not, however, confined to the New Testament. It may be seen at all times of crisis in the Church's life, and never more so than today. Writing of the Churches of the Continent of Europe, Dr. Kraemer, who has since sealed his testimony with his own arrest and imprisonment, says: " They have to fight for their place and existence. In many cases they have become underground Churches or Churches under the Cross. It is impossible to give an adequate idea of the spiritual and physical suffering that statement implies. Nor is it possible to describe the mystery of divine and victorious joy by which this suffering is again and again transformed." So in the life of the Church the suffering of the Redeemer is reproduced, and through the mighty power of his Spirit the victory is won.

Thus from our consideration of the human struggle we have gained a vision of the Captain of man's salvation stooping to the depths of self-identification in order that he might share man's lot and gain the victory over his foes and lead him out into liberty and life; we have caught a glimpse too of redeemed man, inspired by the Spirit of Christ, going forth to bear witness among his fellows to the liberty wherewith Christ has set him free, and opposing the very powers of darkness in the strength of his victory. Was there ever such a day as this for proclaiming that freedom which his victory has procured? Truly it is through that victory alone that the peace for which men long can come to the world.

He is Victor: and in his victory is our liberty and peace.[11]

8. The Cross as Righteous Judgement

"For he hath made him to be sin for us, who knew no sin; that we might be made the righteousness of God in him."
— *II Cor. 5:21.*

No idea has laid more powerful hold upon men's imaginations in recent times than that described by the phrase ' the new order.' Hitler has envisaged his ' New Order ' for Europe; the United Nations on their part are seeking to outline a ' New Order ' for the world. The idea has ' caught on ' because of the widespread feeling that at least during the generation just past there has been no real order at all. Men have become bewildered by reason of the general sense of insecurity and anxious by reason of the lack of any clear definition of man's status within the community. The life of the community in fact has everywhere been decaying and man has become terrified as he has begun to realize the perils of what one writer has graphically called ' noncommunal disintegration.' Man knows that one essential of his life is that it should be shared with others in community; but how to bring order out of chaos and new community out of hatred and antagonism seems beyond his wit to devise.

One thing, however, would be generally agreed — that any possibility of true community life must ultimately depend upon the establishment of authority. Where a central authority is recognized by all, community comes into existence; and history has shown that this authority attains its highest efficacy when it is vested in a living person rather than in an impersonal law. There must be laws, there must be the whole machinery of government; but when beyond all there is a personal embodiment of the authority thus exercised, the community is as strongly established as is possible under the conditions of human life.

I

We may, then, take our knowledge of the human community and the manner of its organization, and use it as a source from which images may be taken to suggest more vividly to our imaginations the essential facts of the Gospel drama outlined in Chapter VI. First of all the relationship between God and men is expressed as that between a ruling king and his subjects. But immediately we ask, What is the nature of this relationship? A little thought will convince us, I believe, that it is always of a double kind: on the one side it makes demands, on the other side it makes promises. In any ordered community a ruler calls for certain duties to be performed and no man is exempt from this call. At the same time he assures his people that while they remain under his just rule, certain privileges will be theirs. Duties and privileges thus constitute the essence of the relationship in which the subject stands to the ruler: or, to use two other words, obligations and rights are the essential elements in any decently ordered community. The two hold together. For whereas it is true, as Jefferson once said, that " man has no natural rights in opposition to his social duties," it is equally true that every man who conscientiously performs his duties is entitled to rights. Community ceases to exist when, as was proclaimed by *Das Schwarze Korps,* the S. S. Storm Troops organ in Germany, on May 14, 1942, " henceforth nobody has rights and everybody has only duties."

We can readily turn to the story of the Garden of Eden in Genesis or the parable of the Wicked Husbandmen in Mark's Gospel to see how this picture of the ruler calling for duties

to be performed but likewise giving the assurance of privileges to be bestowed is used to describe the essential relationship between God and man. But any serious consideration of
the upbuilding of community today would also, I think, in
large measure agree to this essential analysis. In the early part
of 1941 there appeared in the British quarterly magazine
Philosophy an article entitled " Justice: Distributive and Corrective." This paper did not approach the subject with any
religious presuppositions but simply sought to set out a view
of justice acceptable to the mind of today. It began by establishing the necessity of what it called a system of distributive
justice — that is, the creation of a system of rights (and consequently of duties and obligations) according to the principle of ' equality of consideration ' for all. It regarded as
fundamental that man must be given certain rights: that is,
he must be given fields of activity in which he could pursue
his interests without molestation. But it also regarded as fundamental that each man must be granted equality of consideration in relation to his rights and this must necessarily
involve duties and obligations. There must be duties and
obligations within society not only in order that my pursuit
of my interests shall not make it impossible for you to pursue
yours, but in order that I may actually assist you in the pursuit of your interests if those interests are for the good of society as a whole. Thus it appears that in insisting upon the
fact that God as Ruler calls for duties to be performed by all
and grants rights to be enjoyed by all, we are insisting upon
something which is generally acceptable to the conscience of
mankind.

II

We pass now to the next stage. In our framework we stated
that the relationship had been spoiled and broken by the sin

of mankind. How, then, is this to be expressed within the field of Ruler and subjects? It means that the subjects have rebelled against the King, and that their revolt has assumed a double aspect. On the one hand they have refused to fulfil their duties and obligations; on the other hand they have despised the privileges and advantages which should have been theirs.

Taking the second first, it is clear that the contempt or neglect of privileges is linked closely with a false sense of values. Certain rights and advantages may be allowed to each individual within the ordering of a community life but it is always possible that individuals or the whole group will set no store upon what is thus granted but will pine after other apparent goods which at present are not theirs. Thus within the economy of the Garden of Eden the right was granted of eating of the fruit of every tree of the garden; but the tree of the knowledge of good and evil was singled out as sacrosanct — not to be touched by human hands. Yet it was upon this tree that man set his heart. Regardless of all the other privileges which might have been his, the grasping of this fruit became the sole object of his desire. Similarly, when Israel had been brought into the Land of Canaan and had been given the opportunity of enjoying a period of relative rest and prosperity, the people could not rest content. They pleaded for " a place in the sun," for power and prestige in relations with other nations; regardless of what great things God had done for them and was providing for them, their heart was set upon a king who should lead them out to the glory of battle and conquest.

These Biblical examples are typical of the two false values which have captivated men's minds in the modern world — the lust for wealth and the lust for power, acquisitiveness and ambition. We are told on highest authority that the resources of the earth are sufficient to provide subsistence for all; yet, despising a standard of living which is decent and adequate, men burn to acquire more and more, and community life is rendered impossible. Further, there are without doubt enough creative tasks in the world to give a satisfying outlet to the whole flow of the world's energy; yet, despising ordinary work, men are consumed with the desire to obtain positions of power and overlordship, and through bitter faction and rivalry true community life is again made impossible. Man is overassertive of his own rights because at heart he despises the rights and privileges which have actually been granted to him; and thus in relation to God we may regard one aspect of sin as man's contempt of the fundamental human rights which God has freely bestowed upon him.

Turning back to the first aspect which we spoke of, the other way in which we may regard sin in this field is that of the refusal to fulfil duties and obligations. Within the community man has duties to perform towards God and towards his brother; and his duties towards the brother are part and parcel of his duty towards God. In fact, we may say that *direct* duties towards God are comparatively few (the offering of a worthy worship is certainly the chief). Most of his duties towards God man is called upon to perform *indirectly* in his relationships with the world and with his fellow men.

In this regard two principles are being impressed upon us again today by reason of the disasters which have been taking place in the world. One is the principle of reverence for the earth and its resources, the other the principle of the sacredness of the personality of every human being. A particular passage from the Malvern Conference Report has already become famous: " We must recover reverence for the earth and its resources, treating it no longer as a reservoir of potential wealth to be exploited but as a storehouse of divine bounty on which we utterly depend." Regarded in this way, the earth and its resources become the medium through which we may fulfil our duty towards God. Certainly a failure to fulfil these necessary obligations leads to the gradual drying up of earth's bounty, and this in turn has disastrous effects upon man's community life. Even more is it evident that to fail in obligation towards a fellow man is to fail in duty towards God. Wrongs done by man to man, cruelties perpetrated within human society are all to be regarded as wrongs against God, as failures in duty which are owed on behalf of the fellow man who was created in His image. Thus the refusal to fulfil duties and obligations within the community is another aspect of the sin of man against God himself.

III

In the face of such a situation the general conscience of mankind would, I am sure, infer that judgement must be meted out. As Anselm says in his *Cur Deus Homo,* God cannot leave his universe in a state of disorder; and, as the old Greek tragedian insisted, the author of the crime must suffer. There is nothing arbitrary about this, for in his deepest heart man feels it is right. When Jesus appealed to his hearers at the conclusion of the parable of the Wicked Husbandmen, they with one voice gave it as their verdict that the Judge must act and punish. When in Milton's great drama, Samson's father proposes to attempt to bring about his ransom, he replies:

> " Spare that proposal, father; spare the trouble
> Of that solicitation. Let me here,
> As I deserve, pay on my punishment;
> And expiate, if possible, my crime."

When duties have been neglected, rights infringed and privileges despised, appropriate justice must be administered.

This brings us at once, however, to the difficult question of the nature of what is called in the article already referred to ' corrective justice.' There is little doubt that ideas as to its nature have undergone considerable change since the days of Anselm or even since the days of Grotius, and this constitutes in large measure the difficulty that writers on the Atonement find in employing legal metaphors drawn from the literature of the past in order to make clearer the significance of the death of Christ for the reader of today. He has other thoughts about what is the just procedure in the punishment of crime and it is essential that due regard should be paid to these ideas even though they cannot be a final expression of the principles of the divine law.

What, then, is being thought about ' corrective justice ' to-day? Much is being written concerning it in relation to the situation as it will exist after this war. How is a just order to be established? What are the principles which will govern this new order? In particular, if a new order comes into being, how are breaches of the new system to be dealt with? I believe that a study of statements made by responsible leaders of thought and of documents such as have been issued by various commissions could be of real help in showing us how corrective justice is being viewed today.[1] But for my purpose here I would refer again to the article already mentioned, supplementing it by reference to three statements of a more popular kind.

In this article it is insisted that there are two distinct conceptions in corrective justice — reparation and punishment. Now in regard to reparation there seems general agreement on all sides. If rights have been infringed, reparation must be made: either the right must be restored or equivalent compensation must be made. I can illustrate this from three recent articles. In the *Fortnightly Review* of February, 1942, the chairman of a London Juvenile Court wrote a deeply inter-

esting article on " The War and the Young Offender." It was
an enlightened article, which sought to investigate the best
methods of dealing with delinquent children. But the magis-
trate did not have the slightest hesitation in speaking of " the
salutary principle of restitution." The fine, the payment of
costs or damages, is regarded as absolutely just and necessary.
Similarly, an editorial in *The Spectator* of March 13, 1942,
spoke of a stiffening up in the administration of justice in
England. Fines, it said, can be imposed, and " it is emphasized
that they must be at least sufficient to exceed any profit the
offender may have been shown to have made out of the trans-
action [a black-market offence]. Such an increase of penalties
is to be wholeheartedly welcomed." Once more, in relation to
the international situation and the offences of which Germany
has been guilty, Lord Maugham, the former Lord Chancellor
wrote this in June of the year 1943: " There must follow on
German defeat a *restoration in kind*. The pictures, the works
of art, the libraries, the scientific instruments must be returned; or the equivalent must be restored to the lands which
have been despoiled. All things of any description which have
been deliberately destroyed must have compensation in kind
made for them. Stocks of materials which have been looted
must also be made good, so far as such stocks can be found.
This is not revenge, nor is it retribution founded on hatred;
it is the simplest and most obvious form of justice." Thus the
principle of reparation and restitution for the infringement
and contempt of rights and privileges is regarded as entirely
just, even though in some cases it may be felt to be impracti-
cable.

In the matter of punishment the situation is not quite so
simple. However, there are certain things which would be
fairly generally agreed:

1. That punishment should be inflicted only if an act has

been wilful or if there has been gross negligence leading to ignorance of the nature of the act.

2. That the aim of punishment should be to influence behaviour so as to induce the person punished, *and others,* to refrain from acts which violate rights.

That is, there is a growing feeling in the conscience of mankind that punishment should never be vengeful but rather should be remedial. Less and less emphasis is being placed upon the infliction of bodily suffering — it may at times be necessary though, it would seem, only in extreme cases; more and more emphasis is being placed upon such instruments as probation, Borstal, imprisonment of a constructive kind, which can help to reform the individual and yet can be sufficiently unpleasant to help to deter others from the same offences. Thus in England the Departmental Committee on Corporal Punishment, after hearing all the evidence, came to the unanimous conclusion that the judicial whipping of young offenders, both as a reformative factor and as a deterrent, had been proved to be ineffective and should therefore be abolished.

To sum up our conclusions in relation to corrective justice: There seems to be a growing agreement that for the establishment of a just order corrective justice must take the form of:

1. The imposition of a clear demand for reparation and restitution.

2. The withdrawal of privileges (this, after all, is the essence of Borstal and imprisonment) at least for a period, together with a disciplined education in the performance of duties owed to self and to society. These two elements of corrective justice will be seen to correspond to the duties and privileges of distributive justice.

Let us now seek to make the great transition and transfer these thoughts to the relationship between God and men.

God, we have suggested, created man with duties to perform and privileges to enjoy. But man in his sin has refused the duties and despised the privileges. Appropriate justice must be administered and, if what we have just said is right, this will take the form of:

1. The demand for reparation.
2. The withdrawal of privilege.

Man is faced, then, with a call to make a restitution which is beyond his highest capacities to fulfil; at the same time he is necessarily placed within a system of restrictions whose aim is to keep him within bounds and bring home to him the folly of his ways. In other words, he goes through life under the load of a debt which he himself can never pay and bound by disabilities from which he can never escape. To say that God treats man thus is not to contravene the views of justice which receive a general consent today.

IV

Is that, then, all that can be said? Is God content that his Kingdom shall remain in a constant state of frustration, an irremediable state of confusion? The whole message of the Christian Gospel is that such is not the case. God restores his Kingdom, sets up the new order of a new Kingdom, *in and through Jesus Christ*. A radical change is made in the whole situation, and this is what, within this field of the imagination, is meant by the Atonement.

How, then, are we to interpret this as taking place? First as regards reparation. Can one pay for another? Not if we are merely isolated individuals with no relation to one another. But nothing is clearer than that we are *not* isolated individuals, that we are all intimately related to one another; for whereas it is true that community is only possible where there are individuals to form it, it is equally true that " it is only in community that personality can be born and develop." Thus we are all in some measure implicated in the faults of one another and we are all therefore involved in the reparation which man as man is due to pay.[2] As it was said recently in an article on the guilt of Germany, " Germany lived its life in peacetime as a unit, it is fighting the war as a unit and it must pay the price as a unit." This may involve intense suffering for the comparatively innocent but in matters which concern the community no other basis of judgement is possible.

Man, then, is faced with the demand for reparation but this payment he is neither willing nor able to make. Moving as he did within this field of the imagination, Anselm was surely right in saying that man must make satisfaction (which is really the same as reparation) but that only God can. What the Christian Gospel affirms is that out of a pure act of his own good will and grace, God in Christ identified himself with humanity so completely that he was able to make reparation on its behalf.

From the very beginning of Jesus' public ministry this self-identification was manifest. It is particularly evident in the narrative of the baptism. In a book written some years ago on *The Meaning of Baptism*, Dr. C. C. Morrison points out how Jesus wished to enter right into the communal life of his people.

" He felt the sense of solidarity with all men. He was here on a mission of incarnation. He stood on man's level. Knowing no sin, he became sin, that he might redeem mankind. It is as idle, says a great teacher, to tell a wife that she has no need to feel ashamed because her husband is committed for fraud, as to tell Jesus that he need not be baptized because he has no personal guilt. It is precisely in this, his self-identification with men in an initiation into an order of the penitent, that his divine character is disclosed. This is the very spirit of the Messiah." [3]

This identification with the communal life of man continued throughout his ministry. He stood alongside humanity in the debt it owed. He gladly and willingly acknowledged the justice of it. Never was there a human duty which he failed to fulfil. He gave himself unstintingly and unceasingly and finally offered up the only final precious thing a man has — namely, life itself. It was no facile payment that he made: it was the payment of his own very lifeblood. It was no merely individual payment that he made: it was the payment on behalf of the whole humanity which he shared.

But there is the other side, the withdrawal of privilege. As we have already insisted, where privilege has been despised, it must inevitably be withdrawn. It is then, however, that man begins to chafe at the removal of what he regards as his just rights. Yet to all these same restraints and restrictions on human life, to all the disciplines and even disabilities which the life of the community now involves, the Son of God willingly submitted himself. A well-known priest from the East End of London, with intimate experience of work in the slums, was preaching before the University of Cambridge on the conditions which must be fulfilled by anyone who would labour in the task of social uplift there. " The example and demand of Jesus," he said, " and if I read aright of St. Paul, is not for generosity in such a manner and measure that it leaves me in the position of benefactor but an adventure towards community which demands from me the voluntary surrender of privilege and the means of power in such a way that it makes me stand in with those whom I love, prepared to share in the risks that attend such identification." Such a voluntary surrender Jesus made to the uttermost. Nothing surely could surpass the utter renunciation of rights and privileges involved in the experience of dereliction on the cross. Still further we have suggested that a truly corrective justice will insist upon a disciplined education in the performance of duties owed to self and to society. Now it is this aspect of Jesus' human experience which is so finely brought out in The Epistle to the Hebrews. Using daring language which has often caused misunderstanding, the writer of the epistle claims that Jesus learned obedience by the things which he suffered and, being made perfect, became the Author of eternal salvation to all who obey him. What the writer is here urging is that Jesus passed through a truly representative human experience, learning the duties which he as man owed to God and to his fellows, and thereby attaining the fulness of a perfect manhood. He was not exempt from testings and trials, nor was he spared the discipline which all true education involves. Following the pathway of painful experience, he willingly accepted the discipline which God imposes for the re-education of his erring subjects.

Thus from the very midst of humanity Jesus paid the uttermost reparation, he surrendered the uttermost privilege. To say this is not necessarily to reckon in exact terms of quantity and measure. What is affirmed is that Jesus acknowledged in life and death that everything a man has he owes to God — that is duty: and again that everything a man has he derives from God — that is privilege. When God as Holy Ruler was so honoured and justified from within the human community itself, atonement was made and the way was opened for that restoration of fellowship between God and man, which is impossible while inequity prevails. " Where there is inequity there is no fellowship: and fellowship is life and lack of it death." [4]

V

Finally we recognize that although at the cross the Atonement was in one sense completed, in another sense it was only begun. As I see it, the action was God's supreme act of faith in the humanity which he had created.[5] There was always the risk that that atoning action would awaken no response, that men would still continue in their sullen resentment, refusing to acknowledge their indebtedness and cursing at the restraints by which their existence was enclosed. But it was God's faith that if from within humanity at infinite cost he could acknowledge publicly the justice of their estate, then hearts would be awakened, would turn and repent, would become identified with Christ in the whole spirit of his action (that is, in the Holy Spirit), would be saved into the glory of the Kingdom of God. And surely God's faith has been justified. A new humanity has come into existence. At Calvary men have acknowledged their own indebtedness, have confessed that their own desert was nothing other than the dereliction of the cross. They have acknowledged the righteousness of God's holy judgement and in that very acknowledgement have become fit for restoration to that Kingdom whose administration is according to this righteousness alone. But, further, they have identified themselves in boundless gratitude with Christ himself. Their eyes have been opened and they truly see. They have no desire save to be united with him in all that he did. And thereby in that identification they become, in St. Paul's word, justified, reinstated in their privileges in the favour and love of God.

It becomes clear that through this identification the restoration of God's Kingdom in righteousness will be continued in the social life of mankind. For while the administration of human justice is necessary within the world as we know it, human justice alone is powerless to establish the righteousness of God. This can be achieved only by those who, identified with Christ and acting under the guidance of his Spirit, take upon themselves the burden of human sin and acknowledge the justice of the condemnation which must fall upon it under the righteous judgement of God. In one of his great pieces of New Testament exposition, James Denney stresses this principle of life with his usual power:

> " God Himself overcomes evil with good; Christ vanquishes the sin of the world by taking the burden of it on Himself; and if we wish to have part in the same work, there is only the same method open to us. Depend upon it, we shall not make others weep for that for which we have not wept; we shall not make that touch the hearts of others which has not first touched our own. That is the law which God has established in the world; He submitted to it Himself in the person of His Son, and He requires us to submit to it. . . . The hard, proud heart is impotent; the mere official is impotent, whether he call himself priest or pastor; all hope and help lie in those who have learned of the Lamb of God who bore the sin of the world." [6]

Thus our consideration of this field of community life, concerned with the administration of justice, gives us a vision of God's distributive justice, of God's corrective justice, of atonement in terms of reparation and reconstructive punishment, of man's sin being judged and of man himself being justified, of the believer being identified with Christ in his atoning work, and of God's restoring his Kingdom in power and glory through Jesus Christ. I believe that everything points today to a new emphasis in men's thinking upon the nature of justice and order and fellowship. Should we not make capital of this by proclaiming afresh the justice of God, a justice fully and finally revealed in the cross of Calvary, a justice progressively realized in the human community as men are justified by faith and have peace with God through our Lord Jesus Christ? This is the only ultimate justice, and except on the basis of such justice no permanent order can come to the world.

9. The Cross as Creative Suffering

"Verily, verily, I say unto you, Except a corn of wheat fall into the ground and die, it abideth alone: but if it die, it bringeth forth much fruit. He that loveth his life shall lose it; and he that hateth his life in this world shall keep it unto life eternal." — *John 12:24, 25.*

The third field of human activity which we are to consider is that of culture. Within this field the essential feature is the presence of a spirit of creativity; apart from this, no culture worthy of the name can exist. From one angle, indeed, life itself can be regarded as an infinitely varied exercise of creativity. Raw material is provided in abundance by this beneficent universe in which we live and to man is granted what Pascal in striking phrase calls the dignity of causality — he can himself by the exercise of his God-given functions mould his material into new and fascinating forms.

We can see this process at work even in the child who, with sand or mud as his material, delights to create forms which may be crude but yet are of his own making: or who, with sounds as his material, gradually creates forms of speech which, though in large measure mimetic, yet contain some element which may be regarded as peculiarly his own. Thus, in a recent charming published letter to a friend, L. G. Barnard writes:

> " This reminds me that unless you were abnormally dull in your early years (which I am sure was not the case) or were robbed of your childhood (which God forbid) you were once a creative artist. Out of a rag doll, perhaps, you made beauty that the finest china-and-kid of the toymaker's art could not match; out of a trifling pond, an ocean on which ships could be launched for great voyages; out of mud and water from the roadside, pies that no cook could equal in a gas oven " (*The Immortal Child*).

When we come to adult life we find an immense field of activity of a more advanced kind. The workman with his tools creates articles out of wood and stone and metal and ivory; the craftsman makes designs and works them into silk or cotton or wool or skins; the mathematician or the philosopher creates new symbols; the musician operates with instruments and sounds; the poet or writer, in what is perhaps the highest form of creativity, uses words to convey thought and ideas and images, uses them and moulds them into forms which are the noblest monuments of the human race. We probably all know something of the thrill of creation, and none ought to know it more than the preacher. For the preacher is the man whose calling it is to create forms out of the most precious material which this earth provides. His material is the everlasting Gospel, his tools are his full powers of thought and imagination, his object is to create a form which shall be the best possible to convey to other minds and imaginations the glory and beauty of that which he is seeking to portray. Possibly no conception of the preacher's task is greater than that which sets it forth as the work of the creative artist.

I

Life as a whole, then, may be regarded as constant creativity. This thought has been powerfully expressed by the great Russian philosopher-theologian Berdyaev — in fact, it is perhaps his characteristic idea. He speaks of the Creator of the world as the greatest of artists, and of man, being made in the image and likeness of God, as a creator too. Free creativeness, he says, is the creature's answer to the great call of its Creator. Man's creative work is the fulfilment of the Creator's secret will. But perhaps the thought has been even more vividly presented to our minds by a novelist who has already made a name for herself in the realm of theology — Miss Dorothy Sayers. Her most substantial theological work has as its title *The Mind of the Maker*, and is an attempt to speak of the nature of God's creativity by drawing analogies from the nature of the work of the literary artist. In the early part of her book she shows that everybody is a 'maker' in the simplest meaning of the term. We spend our lives putting matter together in new patterns and so 'creating' forms which were not there before. This is so intimate and universal a function of nature that we scarcely ever think about it. In a very real sense all are creators and from one point of view life itself may be looked upon simply as a widely varied exercise of creativity.

But now we must ask the question, what do we mean by creativity? Put in simplest terms, it means surely the making of something new which has *form* and *meaning*. On the one hand, it is not chaotic and formless; on the other hand, it is not irrelevant and meaningless. So in the first chapter of Genesis, beginning with a condition which was without form and void, or, as we might say, chaotic and meaningless, God, by the exercise of his creative word, brought into being a world which had beauty of form and depth of meaning. " God said, Let there be light: and there was light. And God saw . . . that it was good " (Gen. 1:3, 4). It was in fact beautiful, perfect in form; at the same time it was meaningful, for it had a part to play in the finished design. This double aspect is clearly of great importance.

In his learned survey of the *Arts and the Art of Criticism*, Professor Greene, of Princeton, lays it down as a fundamental principle that the true artist must handle with skill both his primary medium (wood, clay, paint, sounds — whatever it may be by which he produces beauty of form) and also his subject matter (physical objects, mental states or imaginative ideas — whatever it may be by which he produces illuminat-

L

ing interpretation). " Both," he says, " await artistic manipulation and success or failure in artistic expressiveness depends entirely upon how both media are handled by the creative artist." [1] Beauty and significance, perfection of form and depth of meaning — these are the two essential qualities of all creative work.

But now we ask the further question, Is it sufficient for the Creator simply to create beautiful and meaningful forms for his own pleasure? The answer of general consent today, just as it is the answer of the Bible itself, would be that it is not sufficient. The Creator desires to share his pleasure with others and that involves the bringing into existence of other creators. For that is a principle of all life — that you cannot really enjoy and understand a thing simply as a spectator. You must in some measure be engaged in the same activity yourself in order to be able to apprehend and appreciate the work of creation. Therefore in the extraordinarily deep and far-reaching words of the Bible, God said, " Let us make man in our image, after our likeness." In other words, God creates a band of creators, a school of disciples. He creates them good and beautiful in form; he creates them with a purpose and meaning to fulfil, to share, namely, in his glorious work of continuous creation.

God, therefore, stands in relation to his people as an artist to his school of pupils, as a master to his disciples, as a pioneering genius to his band of followers. But how are we to analyse this relationship? Once again, it appears, the relationship has a double character. On the one side the teacher or artist demands from these who would follow in his steps intense concentration, discipline, perseverance, humility, teachableness; no teacher believes that anything worth-while can be achieved without hard work. A recent critical study of Walt Whitman, for instance, calls in question his statement that a perfect poem " budded loosely as lilacs and roses on a bush." " Creation," the literary critic writes, " involves intense concentration and the more inevitable a poet's inspiration is the more firmly are his faculties centred in an act. It is by this concentration that he achieves the simplicity which Whitman rightly describes as ' the art of art ' and ' the glory of expression.' " And as Archbishop Temple wrote in an essay some years ago on the nature of education:

> " The first function of the educator is to train the capacity of attention, insisting that the child shall attend to the duty of the moment, whatever that may be, in spite of all sights and sounds which may tend to divert the attention. This faculty of concentration upon the work of the moment is the first and the last business of Education " (*Mens Creatrix*, p. 227) .

But while the teacher will ever be unyielding in his insistence upon the need for toil, yet he will be equally encouraging in his promise of growing facility and ultimate achievement; and further he will pledge his own guidance and interest and approval and even a subtle impartation of his own spirit to one who will dwell in his company and seek instruction at his hand. It is in this connection an interesting fact that the very word ' professor,' so prominent in the educational world today, has its origin in the promises which teachers in the ancient world were wont to make to their pupils. Demands and promises may not figure largely in modern methods, but they form the essence of the classical relationship between teacher and learner, and I am inclined to think that we should achieve greater results in education today by a return to something of this kind.

II

Such, then, is the ideal relation, and man is called upon to follow God in the creation of that which is beautiful and meaningful. But there is another side to the picture. This relation has been spoiled and marred, first, by man's passivity, sloth and vagrancy: he refuses to engage in the discipline and application which are necessary for creative achievement. It is spoiled, secondly, by his self-confidence and pride, which lead him to reject all guidance and to be indifferent to any possible inspiration and reward which might come to him from his relationship with the Master. This is sin within this field of the imagination — it is essentially sloth and presumption. It is an unwillingness to yield to toil and travail in the present, or it is an unwillingness to accept guidance and direction for the future.

Let us seek to illustrate these two aspects of human sinfulness. For the first there is the vivid parable of our Lord in which talents are given to men to enable them to exercise their creative abilities. Two of them labour under the stimulus of the memory of their Master's spirit and of the expectation of their Master's reward. The third, however, refuses to give himself to toil and discipline: he is slothful and indolent — and buries his talent in the earth where it becomes formless and meaningless. He yields himself up, in other words, to the earth-spirit, the spirit of self-indulgence, the spirit of the world, the flesh and the Devil. Here is one form of sin in this field of the imagination, and it has been vividly revealed to us in the life of the last twenty-five years. More and more men have sought to escape from life's discipline and to yield themselves up to self-pleasing and self-indulgence. I read recently a criticism of France which Matthew Arnold made even in his day — that she had given herself up to the worship of the great goddess Lubricity. That may be an exaggeration but certainly in the last twenty-five years there has been an orgy of self-indulgence on the part of her leaders, with a refusal to concentrate on the real business of the welfare of the nation. Then again, among the Anglo-Saxon peoples after the last war there went up the cry for self-expression, which was not an expression of the true self but a surrender to the dark underworld of the earth-spirit and the subconscious mind. And one result has been the so-called art and creativity of this period in which meaningless objects have been multiplied by mass production and meaningless music has been bleated forth by jazzers and crooners, and meaningless words have been strung together in endless lines by a new school of literary men.

Then let us consider the other side. This is perhaps nowhere more vividly illustrated than in the powerful story of the Tower of Babel. There we see human self-confidence and pride in its fullest manifestation. " Go to, let us build us a city and a tower, whose top may reach unto heaven; and let us make a name, lest we be scattered abroad upon the face of the whole earth." Instead of squandering his creative ability and submerging it in the earth, man concentrates it and exalts it to heaven. He is guilty of that sin which even the old Greeks were terrified of committing — the sin of *hubris,* or excess. For them all life was the same. It would begin in beauty and frailness, grow in strength, grow too strong or too proud, and then inevitably dwindle and die. The same lesson is enforced by Mr. Arnold Toynbee with telling power as he surveys the rise and fall of human civilizations. They are generated, they progress through the stimulus of challenge, overreach themselves through *hubris* and presumption and then sink into decline. How foolish proud man becomes in the possession of power! " Who that has lived many years on this earth," writes Professor MacIver, " can have failed to observe how even a modicum of irresponsible power perverts the intelligence and hardens the sensibilities, how the jack-in-office struts in pompous undiscerning pride, how the bureaucrat loses touch with humanity, how the petty boss, when no superior watches, becomes a wretched bully? In every sphere of human activity, in the factory, in the trade-union, in the home, in the church, in the barracks, in the prison, even in the seats of learning, let power be uncontrolled and it will work the same effects. With some of his bitterest words Shakespeare characterized this phenomenon:

> " ' Man, proud man,
> Drest in a little brief authority,
> Most ignorant of what he's most assured,
> His glassy essence, like an angry ape,
> Plays such fantastic tricks before high heaven
> As make the angels weep.' " [2]

Truly if the Devil cannot sap man's creative energies by inducing him to surrender them to the demons of earth, he will drive him to his ruin by inducing him to employ them in mounting to the sky. Here is man, then, as creator and created — sinning on the one side in degrading his creatorship, sinning on the other side in repudiating his createdness.

Thus in this field of the imagination we see a world which has in St. Paul's words fallen short of the glory of God, failed to achieve that creation of a beautiful and meaningful cosmos which was, the Creator's purpose; we see at the same time a world which, again in St. Paul's phrase, has grown vain in its own imaginations and has worshipped and served the creature rather than the Creator who is blessed forever. We see in fact a world from which meaning has disappeared and which is empty of true creative life. There is again no hope unless the whole situation be changed by a new creative act of God himself.

It is the glory of the Christian Gospel to proclaim that God has entered into this situation in Christ to re-create and renew and — this surely is important — to make the splendour of the Re-creation even more wonderful than that of Creation itself. This is the process which, within this field of the imagination, we call the Atonement.

III

How, then, are we to conceive the outworking of this process? How, we may ask, would a teacher who is also a creative artist, deal with such a situation? He is faced with a body of recalcitrant pupils, indolent and self-assured, who are not only hostile to himself but who also have marred and spoiled his work. He might well give them up entirely and begin a completely new work; but instead he may see in that very situation which confronts him an opportunity for a creative achievement which will surpass in splendour anything hitherto known.

Let us assume then that he adopts the latter course. How is he to create a work of art out of material which is not passive and inert but active and volitional? To force the material into some preconceived pattern is not to produce a work of art. Surely the essential art of the true teacher is to stimulate the willing response of the pupil by setting forth a model, an example, which shall at once challenge and guide him to a true expression of his own inner self. By this means the teacher will not only enable the pupil to produce a work of art by his own labour; he will also bring into being a character which is at once beautiful and meaningful.

The teacher's primary purpose, then, is to create beautiful and meaningful characters and to do this he will first set forth a model or example which is to act as the creative norm. Into the production of this model he will pour the very maximum of his own intensity and passion and, as we suggested earlier, he will work, first, with an idea or principle — that is his subject matter — and, secondly, with certain raw material which is the medium of the expression of his art.

Transferring all this to the sphere of God's relations with man, we ask first what is the idea or principle which is to be embodied in what we have called the new model or example. To me it is clear that the idea or principle is that which in some mysterious way seems to lie at the very heart of the universe — the principle that only through death can richer life come into existence. Think how this principle seems to suffuse the universe as we know it. It is fundamental in Nature. In a fascinating book entitled *The Discipline of Peace*, Mr. K. E. Barlow shows how utterly man is dependent upon the soil for his physical existence, and, indeed, for his general welfare. It is literally true to say that man's continued existence on this earth is possible only so long as the soil maintains its strength and fertility. But what are the processes which keep the soil ' in good heart '? " Year by year the seasonal fall of the leaf, the rotting of stems and roots, the excreta of animals and in some cases their carcases, fall upon the soil and are rotted by the activities of a host of insects and bacteria. The product which eventually results from this disintegration is the humus. This humus is the main source of the food which feeds plant life, although certain minerals are drawn from the inorganic materials of the soil and from the weathering of rock. Humus is thus the pivot of a living cycle. The covering of vegetation provides the stems and roots which are rotted down to humus. At the same time humus feeds the growth of stem and root." In other words, at the basis of all organic existence there is this constantly renewed process of life through death.

But again this principle seems to be fundamental in human thought. Few things are more remarkable in the history of man than the way in which, the world over, there has been the thought that only through sacrifice in some shape or form could life be renewed and strengthened. The exact rationale of the institution of sacrifice is notoriously difficult to determine, but the motive of life-renewal is certainly one of the most prominent in its history. It is as if there were a certain

invisible substratum of life which, like the soil, needed constantly to be repaired, refreshed and renewed and that the
means to this end were to be found in the blood poured out
in sacrifice. Certainly, as the book of Leviticus so clearly tells
us, the life of the flesh is in the blood, and it is by the shedding
of this blood that a kind of spiritual ' humus ' is formed which
fertilizes the whole substratum of human existence. And even
when the material form of sacrifice is abandoned and man
pours himself out in some more spiritual way for the sake of
a larger whole, still there is the dim sense in his heart that only
through his sacrifice can the larger entity out of which he
himself originally sprang continue to survive.

This principle of life through death is one of the great mys-
teries of the universe but it is one which cannot possibly be
denied.

" And all through life I see a cross —
    Where sons of God yield up their breath;
  There is no gain except by loss;
    There is no life except by death."

And it was this idea or principle which, we affirm, was the subject matter of the new work of the divine Artist.

What, then, was to be his material? The raw material was
surely nothing other than the stuff of human living, the experiences and events of daily existence. Of this material there
had to be the complete mastery. No artist can achieve perfection of form apart from a veritable wrestling with his material and a determination to master the technique associated
with it. To Goethe, for instance, there came the idea of his
song of Creation; but then for twelve long years he became
absorbed in scientific study, seeking to discover everything
possible about the way in which the present world came into
existence. So it was necessary for the divine Artist likewise
to immerse himself in the human material at his command;

in other terms, the Word had to become flesh, the Creative Idea had to be embodied in truly human form, that so the perfect Model or Example might be set forth before the eyes of men.

IV

Bearing this analysis in mind, we can fill in the picture of what the Atonement means in terms of images taken from the field of creative culture. The idea of fulness of life only through death is, I believe, one of the dominant thoughts in the mind of Jesus as revealed to us in the Gospel record. From the time of the baptism onwards, it sounds like a deep basic tone through the whole of the Gospel symphony. It is the controlling spirit of his life and only reaches its natural and inevitable expression in the climax of Calvary.

I need only mention the way in which this primary idea was worked out in every detail of Jesus' life. The general pattern became clear as early as at the time of the temptation in the wilderness. There, surely, the whole process of his life was already vivid to his imagination; it was an experience comparable to the beginning of a poet's inspiration, when the outline of his creative work frames itself in his mind. This part of the poet's work is described so strikingly in a passage quoted by Mr. Herbert Read in his valuable introduction to the theory of modern painting and sculpture that I beg leave to transcribe the words in order that they may be considered in this present context. They are taken from De Sanctis' *History of Italian Literature* and occur in a passage describing Dante's first conceptions of his *Divine Comedy:*

" The early time of a poet's inspiration — that tentative time which is so highly dramatic — is hidden to criticism. It is the time of silent contest of the poet with himself, of vague outlines, of coming and going in his mind; it is the intimate history of the poet. When a subject comes into the brain of a creative writer, it at once dissolves that part of reality which suggested it. The earthly images seem to fluctuate, like objects in a mass of vapour seen from above. The figures — the trees, the towers, the houses — disintegrate, become fragmentary. To create reality, a poet must first have the force to kill it. But instantly the fragments draw again together, in love with each other, seeking one another, coming together with desire, with the obscure presentiment of the new life to which they are destined. And the first real moment of creation in that tumultuous and fragmentary world is the moment when those fragments find a point, a centre around which they can press. It is then that the poet's creation comes out from the unlimited, which makes it fluctuant, and takes on a definite form — it is then that it comes to birth. It is born and lives, or rather it develops gradually, in conformity with its essence " (pp. 74, 75) .

Is not this exactly what we see going on during those forty creative days in the wilderness — the reality of human life as Jesus knew it being dissolved, disintegrated, even killed, but then instantly the fragments coming together again around " a point, a centre around which they can press," and that point a cross? A new pattern of living was born through that experience and we see Jesus coming forth to live as man amongst men, encountering every situation of human life and, without a trace of self-indulgence or self-sufficiency, exercising his creative art in relation to it. For what does he do with each situation? He grapples with it, negates it, brings it to its death, that so it may be transformed into something new as it becomes vitally related to his own Person. In words used by E. Stanley Jones in another context, " He lays hold on the raw materials of human living, pleasure and pain, compliment and criticism, justice and injustice, and takes them up into the purpose of His life, as the lotus takes the muck and mire and transforms it into the beauty of the lotus flower." [3] So we proceed through the Gospels, following along no smooth and easy road but at the same time a road of majestic re-creation. It is a literally continuous re-creation of discord into harmony, of tragedy into triumph, of resistance into energy. It is the making of life into a great symphony, a great poem, a great drama in which the key idea is that of the transfiguration of the discordant and ugly into the beautiful and harmonious.

Yet what will he do with suffering, that constant impediment to all human hopes and ambitions? What will he do with death, that unyielding tyrant who finally judges man's indolence and *hubris* and brings all man's schemes of creation to nought? What will he do with a cross, that ugliest symbol of the ancient world, which signified only blood and cruelty? What will he do with it? He will wrestle with it, lay hold of it, lift it up into his mighty passion, transfigure it, re-create it, make it an integral part of the most glorious and beautiful creation which this world can conceive. So on the night of his betrayal, he takes the creative idea and presents it vividly to his pupils in dramatic form; on the next day he goes forward to make that idea actual and visible upon the plane of history in the cross of Calvary. Is it to be wondered at that the Creation hymn is even surpassed by the Re-creation hymn? "Worthy is the Lamb that was slain to receive the power, and the riches, and the wisdom, and the might, and the honour, and the glory, and the blessing."

V.

It is in this way, then, in the third field of the imagination that we conceive of the Atonement being made. The Perfect Example, manifesting the full beauty and meaning of life, is now before men's eyes. Like a poet, Jesus has made the shape and meaning of life, to use the words of a recent writer, visible and ardent. Not merely are we confronted with words and maxims for, to quote again from E. Stanley Jones, " if good maxims could save a people, China would be the most saved nation in the world, for whole streets of China are filled with good mottoes on them. But they have no power to regenerate for the Word has never become flesh. Only when it does become flesh, does it shake us like a passion and make us new." [4] The Word of the eternal sacrifice has become flesh and the new Spirit — the eternal Spirit by which he offered himself without spot unto God — has been manifested within the human scene.[5] Moreover — and this is of high importance — the Example of which we have spoken was not of the kind which is sometimes referred to as a bare or naked example. It was not an example remote from men's actual life; nor was it an example unrelated to the living power of God. Rather was it an example set in the very heart of humanity yet vibrant with the very life of God himself. It was, in other words, an *efficax symbolum,* an effectual sign, a dynamic example, of the quality of the ' prophetic symbol ' which Dr. Wheeler Robinson describes so admirably in his various writings. It helped to bring about that which it represented. It was now embedded in human life, the seed of that new humanity whose essential pattern was no longer to be Creation alone but Creation — Death — Re-creation, a pattern derived from the Example of the incarnate Son of God which acts as its generative power. In yielding himself up to that Spirit, in identifying himself and all his creative energies with that great dramatic process of Re-creation which God undertook on his behalf, man attains his true destiny and finds his life, his art, his whole culture being transfigured into a new glory by the creative spirit of God.

This is the wonder of the Christian religion, that it is shot through and through with this motif of a richer life emerging out of tragedy and death. Its greatest music, its greatest poetry, its greatest drama, all are inspired by this same sequence, Creation — Passion — Re-creation. The late Archbishop Söderblom did not hesitate to give the name of 'the fifth Gospel' to the musical interpretation of the story of redemption which reaches its highest point in Johann Sebastian Bach. Surely it is no chance happening that one of the great masterpieces of music — to some, the summit of all musical expression — the " Credo " in the " Mass in B Minor," has as its essential theme the glory of Creation coming to its triumphant fulfilment by way of the passion of the cross. Surely, again, it is not by chance that one of the greatest dramas of literature, Milton's *Samson Agonistes* likewise has as its theme a life of magnificent promise coming to a true fulfilment only through bitter suffering and loss. Once more, it is surely significant, as Lord David Cecil has recently pointed out, that within this time of war Mr. T. S. Eliot seems to be the one writer who has gained in stature. For, as he goes on to say, Mr. Eliot is a Christian and Christianity accepts suffering and transmutes it. Life in its evil as well as its good, in its frustration as well as its fulfilment, can be the expression of the divine will, the fleeting shadow of a divine and eternal Spirit.

Moreover, what is true for the individual is also true for society: it can only be renewed and regenerated by the way of the cross. Nowhere, I think, has this been more powerfully stated than by the anonymous author 'Nicodemus' in his book *Midnight Hour*. He confesses at the beginning that he decided to make public his own inner wrestlings and agonies of soul, only because of his conviction that society at large could be transformed by no other way than by that which had brought about his own personal renewal of life. The significance of this self-revelation for the corporate life of mankind is admirably brought out by Mr. R. Gregor Smith in his deeply sympathetic commentary in the Christian News-Letter: two sections in particular make clear how utterly relevant is the pattern of crucifixion and resurrection to the social problems which face us today, and I propose to quote them in full:

" The only possible humanity is the one depicted in Nicodemus himself, the one that is condemned and shattered by God's judgement and then re-integrated through Christ into life with God. This is what Nicodemus, following Kierkegaard, calls the way ' through death to life, the way of despair in all merely human achievements, the way of a new birth. Only when this has really taken place is there the possibility of undertaking effective action for the need of society.

" This analysis is derived from the life of Christ. Christ's life is the embodiment of this action, first the negative and solitary experience of denial of the world, detachment from life and hatred of the world, and then the positive and corporate experience of affirmation of the world, attachment to life, and love of all men. The movement of Christ's life from the perfection of society in the ' bosom of the Father ' through the fallen world back to that perfection involves the Cross. The bridge between life with God and the integration of the life of society is, therefore, the crucified God-man. This is a permanent fact of history, and in our own individual lives as well as in the life of the Church and of the whole human community there must be the same paradoxical loss of life and dying with Christ in order to save life and live with God. The crucified Christ is the living statement of God's demand on all society. The Cross of Christ characterizes the way of regeneration for all society." [6]

Finally, then, from our consideration of the cultural life of man we have gained a vision of the Re-creator who by his own suffering and death constituted a new pattern of existence and set a new creative spirit to work within the individual and social life of mankind. Much is being said today about the decline of the West, the end of an epoch, the death of an old civilization. Here surely is the only way of renewal and recovery — a humble self-abasement at the foot of the cross, a grateful self-fulfilment through the re-creative Spirit of Christ.

" If any man be in Christ, there is a new creation: old things are passed away; behold, all things are become new."

10. The Cross as Forgiving Love

"Greater love hath no man than this, that a man lay down his life for his friends." — *John 15:13.*

The last field of human activity which we have to consider is that which is centred in the home. The organization of the family has shown wide variations at different periods of history but it has always tended to fasten upon some relatively settled location as the centre of its life. This is the home which provides shelter and protection and at the same time is the common meeting-ground for the various members of the family group.

One difficulty may present itself to our minds at once: it may be said that there is little to distinguish this field from that of the community which we considered at an earlier stage. Thus a recent writer, speaking of the paramount need of having an active Christian community both as a setting and as a focus for Christian teaching, goes on to say that the home provides just such a community — "the nearest approach, indeed, to the Kingdom of Heaven which we experience on earth." [1] Another writer likewise asserts that the only real home is a small commonwealth in which each "gladly gives according to his ability and gratefully receives according to his needs." [2] Thus the terms community, kingdom, and commonwealth, which we should have unhesitatingly assigned to the second area of life that we considered, are here applied in different ways to the home and the family which it contains.

Yet almost instinctively we feel that there is a real difference between the more limited group which we call the family and the wider group which we call the clan or tribe or nation.

There are, of course, similarities which lead to the occasional interchange of terms belonging primarily to one or other of these areas of life. But in general the home and the family stand for something more intimate, more flexible, more tender, more directly personal. The blood bond is much closer and the relationships between man and woman, between adult and child, take an altogether more prominent part in the home than in the wider life of the organized community. Thus it is, we believe, legitimate to isolate this field of human activity and to take from it the images and concepts which it provides for our particular purpose.

I

In the first place, then, we ask what is the fundamental relationship which we associate with the life of the family. There can be only one answer — it is the relationship of love. One solitary bond is sufficient to unite man and woman, parent and child — it is the bond of love. To use the phrase of the writer already quoted, the home must be " the little kingdom ruled by Love." [3] And herein lies a notable distinction from the life of the community; for whereas in that field justice is regarded as the first essential, here without a doubt the first essential is this great and mysterious quality which we call love.

But to say this is not to supply a final answer. What is the nature of true love? Few words have been so debased as this has been; infatuation, sentiment, a passing attraction, softness, an undiscriminating kindliness, even lust itself, have been clothed with this regal word love. It is, therefore, imperative that we should first seek to gain a true idea of what love really means. But in order to do this we cannot remain simply in the realm of the abstract; we must pass over to the realm of the concrete and personal. Love is that relationship existing between a lover and a loved one, between man and woman, between mother and child, between father and child, between children themselves. We might seek to analyse any one of these relationships but we are bound to recognize that the Bible itself fastens upon one as being supremely relevant to its own revelation of the nature of the relationship between God and men. It does, indeed, speak in a remarkable way of the love of God to Israel and the love of Christ to his Church as being comparable to the love of a husband for his wife. Moreover, in passages of great beauty and tenderness, it speaks of God's heart of love for his children as being like that of a mother for her own. These relationships are certainly not to be excluded from any comprehensive account of the nature of love. Yet it is a fact that the relationship on which the Bible lays the altogether supreme emphasis is that which exists between father and son. Applied to the relationship of Jehovah and Israel in the Old Testament, it comes to its fullest expression in the perfect relationship between the Father and the Son in the New, a relationship which it is God's purpose to reproduce as far as is possible in the lives of those who themselves are drawn into a fellowship of faith with the Son of his love. Possibly the most adequate of all analyses of love would be a combination of the qualities inherent in fatherhood and motherhood. But for simplicity's sake and in view of the Biblical emphasis, we shall focus our attention upon the relationship between father and son.

As in the other relationships which we have considered, we find that here a double aspect is to be seen. On the one side there is a ceaseless and unbounded self-giving. There is what Dr. Clow calls an " insight and sympathy which craves to bless," " a quenchless desire for the well-being of the beloved." [4] Or, as he expresses it in a striking paradox, " it is that sense of need which can be satisfied only by giving." The father must give himself unsparingly to provide shelter, nourishment, protection, guidance, encouragement, assistance, the best he has, for the sake of the child, if he is to be in the least worthy of the name father. This side of the relationship would hardly be challenged today. However our practice may fall short of the ideal, instinctively we feel that one who has been responsible for the generation of a human life must hold himself responsible for tending and nurturing that life until it reach its maturity; and that must involve a sustained and unstinted process of self-communication.

But there is another side. It has been pointed out that certainly in New Testament times the primary note associated with fatherhood was that of authority. The relationship involves demand, a measure of obligation, the imposition of a standard and ideal. This does not mean that within the family a situation should develop where, as Mr. Sidney Dark vividly puts it, " the father and mother issue orders in the parlour as though they were strutting a quarterdeck." [5] Nor does it mean that fatherhood can allow the exertion of a bare authority, a mere arbitrariness dependent on the whim of an undisciplined character. But it does mean that a father, if he is to be worthy of the name, must seek to bring his son into conformity with a certain ideal of character and conduct which he has himself learned during the course of his own experience of life. How he will do this we are not concerned at the moment to enquire. But that this demand for conformity is an essential element of true fatherhood seems to us self-evident.

The point is so important that reference may be made to two important discussions of it — one recent and one in an older book which still stands perhaps as the classic exposition of the doctrine of the Fatherhood of God. In the latter, Dr. John Scott Lidgett is insisting that to speak of the Fatherhood of God does not lead to the exclusion of his judicial functions. In fact, he goes on, if God is truly love, he must maintain the integrity and consistency of his own holy character and must likewise maintain the consistency and integrity of that constitution and order of the universe which proceeds from him. For, looking at human life in general, Lidgett affirms:

" Men may appear able to maintain the integrity of their own character, while indifferent to the conduct of their fellow-men. But the appearance is deceptive; for, directly other men are brought into immediate contact with me in the complex and manifold relations of life, I can only maintain the integrity of my character by demanding and enforcing, to the utmost of my power, integrity in them. There is no surer way of losing character than the cowardice which shrinks from demanding character in others." [6]

This leads him to conclude that all true fatherhood has its judicial side:

" It may be in abeyance, or it may come forward into sharp and even exclusive manifestation. Yet, even when it is sharpest and most exclusive, it is — if true to its office — dominated by the fatherly motive, and exercised simply to vindicate and to secure the integrity of the family bond, in the sacred interests of life and love. To sever at any time the claims of justice from the interests of life and love, is to destroy justice by perverting it to unreason and cruelty; and, on the other hand, nothing can make justice so rigorous and unsparing as the fact that the safeguarding of life and love is committed to its care." [7]

The more recent discussion to which I refer is found in the notable book by Mr. C. S. Lewis, *The Problem of Pain*. There he has an impressive chapter on the divine goodness which seeks to show, by means of human analogies, that true love cannot be indifferent to the quality of the life of the beloved. He readily admits that we are all inclined to hanker after

" not so much a Father in Heaven as a grandfather in heaven — a senile benevolence who, as they say, ' liked to see young people enjoying themselves.' " But such a concept really involves a contempt of the beloved object — in fact it is not really love or fatherhood at all. So he goes on to suggest that even an artist with an artifact or a man with a beast will take infinite pains to bring it into conformity with a certain standard, not because he loves it a little, but because he loves it much. Even more will a father do the same with his son. The father must use his authority " to make the son into the sort of human being he, rightly, and in his superior wisdom, wants him to be." " A father half apologetic for having brought his son into the world, afraid to restrain him lest he should create inhibitions or even to instruct him lest he should interfere with his independence of mind is a most misleading symbol of the Divine Fatherhood." [8] The whole chapter is well worth study. It lays striking emphasis upon the point we are seeking to establish, that true fatherhood must involve a demand for conformity of character; it is summed up, perhaps, in part of a quotation with which the chapter begins, " Love can never be reconciled to an unlovely object." [9]

II

We can, therefore, insist upon these as the two essential qualities of fatherhood: first, a ceaseless and unbounded self-outpouring and, secondly, a constant and imperative self-affirming by means of inexorable demand. For a human father this demand should rest, not upon his own whim or fancy, but upon the revealed character of God himself; only in the case of the Fatherhood of God can the demand rest upon the character of the one who makes it.

We pass now to investigate the nature of sin as conceived

within this field of human relationships. The son can mar
and spoil the relationship, and that in two ways. On the one
hand, he may despise or be indifferent to the self-giving of
the father; on the other hand, he may claim his independence
and reject any demand for conformity to a standard which the
father may impose. I suppose the classic examples of the first
attitude are those evinced by the two brothers in the parable
of the Prodigal Son. Some of the most moving words in the
whole of the Bible describe the constant attitude of the father: " Son, thou art ever with me, and all that I have is
thine." All that I have is thine — that is the measure of the
father's self-giving to each of the sons. Yet the first cares so
little that his only desire is to possess the impersonal goods
and to be rid of the personal giver; the second cares so little
that he utterly fails to recognize the true nature of the giving
and is only intent upon grasping something which he has not
yet enjoyed. An utter failure to appreciate the father's self-
giving and an insatiable desire to enjoy *things* and sensuous
delights rather than the personal communion which he was
willing so freely to bestow — such is the sin of unworthy sonship as we see it in that vivid parable.

As regards the second attitude, examples from history are
all too common. Often, no doubt, it is due to the fatal tendency on the part of those of us who are fathers to demand a
standard from our sons which we are not prepared to accept
for ourselves or to ask from them obedience to certain rules of
behaviour which have no justification in any higher order of
things. If we do this, we cannot complain if the sons take their
own way and refuse to submit to demands which outrage their
sense of what is just and right. But although we are often to
blame, it is not always so; and certainly in the case of God and
his children there can be no predisposing cause on his side
for the action of man. Ever consistent with his own standard
of holiness, asking from men only that they shall walk in con-

formity with that image in which they were created, he is yet faced with the flat contradiction of the filial spirit of dependence and with the blank refusal to accept as the standard of life the holy character of the Father who begat them. Men resent discipline and rebel against the will which imposes it.

The results of sin so conceived are clear. By craving for the gifts while despising the Giver, the son gradually becomes bound up with material things until he finds himself unable to break free from them. He who was destined to be the heir of the world, to exercise spiritual lordship over all his father's possessions, becomes, instead, the slave of the world. As Dr. Scott Lidgett says, he becomes the tool and victim, instead of the possessor, of his earthly life. He has deliberately departed to the far country and is there the dupe of his companions and the prisoner of his circumstances. In addition, he who has rejected the demand for conformity to the character of the higher does not simply remain on the same level but gradually sinks to conformity to the character of the lower. He who rejects the superhuman inevitably moves towards the subhuman; he who departs from the divine moves towards the demonic; he who repudiates the beautiful is well on his way to the bestial. The man who turns his back upon the high standards of the father, finds himself, like the prodigal, seated finally amidst the degradation and squalor of the beasts and grubbing amongst the husks. No picture in all literature so vividly portrays the results of unfilial response to a father's love as does that of the miserable prodigal living in the far country in the midst of the swine.

III

How, then, can the situation be changed? How can sinful children be reconciled to an earthly father? How, above all, can sinful men be reconciled to a Heavenly Father? The message of the Christian Gospel is that God was reconciling the world to himself in Christ, that the Father was reconciling men to himself in the Son. Let us consider reconciliation in the field of family relationships and seek to have our imaginations quickened in this way.

Certain things we can lay down as fundamental within the sphere of true family life. In the first place, the father is not concerned primarily with exacting a penalty when an attitude such as we have described has been manifested by the son. A father may under certain circumstances be compelled to demand that reparation be made or punishment inflicted; but in these cases he is acting more in his capacity as head of the little commonwealth than as father to the child. For example, if the child has done wrong to another member of the family, or to someone outside the family, he must make reparation in some form and the father will often be the one whose duty it is to see that this is done. But he is not, we repeat, in those cases acting primarily within the father-son relationship. If the child's sin has been in the form which we have described above — despising the father's love and refusing to conform to the father's ideal of character — then it is not reparation or penalty which concerns the father; rather, it is penitence, confession, an entire change of attitude, a true desire for the restoration of the relationship of confidence and trust which should exist between father and son.

Further, we may say that the father's way of dealing with the estranged son must necessarily be exceedingly cautious. Family relationships, being the most intimate, are like fine and delicate machinery — they can be readjusted only by a most delicate touch. The child may be restored to some kind of obedience or subserviency by rougher methods; but if the restoration is to be to *sonship,* infinite care and patience must be shown. This surely is one of the marks of genius of the parable of the Prodigal Son. The father might easily have pursued the son to the far country and dealt with him in the midst of his misery; but though the prodigal might have welcomed the succour thus provided, there would have been no guarantee that his fundamental disposition would have changed. Any suggestion of forcing himself upon the son, of leaving him no alternative but to accept the proffered succour, is entirely absent from the father's dealings. Unless there be a restoration to the free relationship of father and son, there will be no real restoration at all.

Such things may be said in a general way and may lead us towards a true picture of what the Atonement stands for in this field of thought. Our affirmation of faith is that God the Son, dwelling from all eternity in the perfect relation to God the Father, of mutual giving and receiving, came forth and so identified himself with sinful humanity that he was able to live the life of perfect Sonship even under the handicaps and disabilities of sinful human existence. On the one hand it was a real sojourn within the human family. Born of a woman, born under the law whereby human life is disciplined, growing to maturity within an ordinary family circle, not ashamed to regard those about him as his brethren, tempted in all points like as we are, learning obedience by the things which he suffered — such was his life, and it was such as to give him a rightful place within the human family. At the same time it was a life without sin. There was never a suggestion of despising the Father's self-giving. Never was there the slightest evidence of being bound up with the gifts and ignoring the Giver. The things of earth he appreciated and rejoiced in but only as gifts from the Father's hand. He ever sat lightly by them and saw beyond them to the Father's own self-giving, of which they were a token and sacrament. He never asked to possess them as his own or to employ them for his own benefit and advantage. Thus from beginning to end he was without sin in his attitude to material things. Moreover, it was a life without sin in that there was never a trace of resentment at the standard of life demanded or the discipline of life by which that standard was to be attained. Earthly sons feel that the standard is unreasonable or that the discipline is unbearable and they grow resentful and rebellious. Not so in his case. To read the Fourth Gospel is to have before one's eyes the picture of a Son who delighted in the holiness of his Father and willingly accepted all the disciplines of earth, even to the point of tasting treachery and bitter jealousy and hatred from those who were his brothers within the human family. He accepted all and still could say: " Father, glorify thy name "; " The cup which my Father hath given me, shall I not drink it?" He experienced the worst suffering which members of the human family could inflict and still could say, " Father, forgive them; for they know not what they do."

IV

What place, then, does the *death* of Christ hold in this field? On the one side it is the final and unmistakable proclamation to men that Sonship does not consist in the abundance of things which he possesses nor in the multitude of forces which he has under his control; these were the interpretations of Sonship proposed by the Devil in the wilderness and Jesus, having refused them by word of mouth then, refused them in a final confessional act upon the cross of Calvary. Though everything earthly were removed, even physical life itself, yet something of infinite worth still remained, namely, the assurance of the Father's good pleasure and love. To borrow a title from Dr. Forsyth, the cross is the ' Great Confessional,' the final affirmation from within humanity that nothing matters save the Father's word and the Father's will.

On the other side the cross is, if I may coin a phrase, the
' Great Intercessional.' Sonship does not inevitably and auto-
matically bring in its train good treatment and warm affec-
tion from the other members of the human family. The
standard of love for the brethren which Sonship necessarily
imposes may seem impossible of fulfilment in face of the injury and wrong which those brothers inflict. In fact, that
injury may lead to resentment of the Father's standard and
a refusal to attempt to continue within it. Why be troubled
any longer by those who are beyond love; why regard them
any longer as brothers within the one family? Why cannot
Sonship be enjoyed without any sense of responsibility or
care for those who are unworthy of the name of brother?

Such is the human reaction, but not the reaction of Christ.
In Principal R. S. Franks's fine words:

" Jesus in His search for the lost was found where they
were. It was not only that he mixed with them, ate with
them, lived with them. All this He might have done without spiritual contact. We come near to others in *sympathy*. Jesus understood the temptation of the sinful; He
knew their evil case. His heart melted for their alienation from the Father and from Himself. We get a glimpse
into His feeling in the sad words: ' O Jerusalem, Jerusalem, how often would I have gathered thy children as
a hen gathers her chickens under her wings, and ye would
not.'

" The approach of Jesus to sinners brought upon Him
all sorts of sufferings, bodily and spiritual. He met with
harsh words, hateful looks, fierce attacks, actuated by mal-
ice, treachery and cruelty. But He went on with His work
of love, teaching, warning, pleading, till at last the sinners
whom He came to save by drawing them to the Father,
rose up against Him, mocked, scourged and crucified
Him. It was the best proof of love that, when faced with
the utmost energy of sinful resistance to the Divine will
of love, He did not withdraw or try to escape or deviate by
one hair's breadth from His course. He simply persevered

in loving men as God loves them. The cry from the Cross in St. Luke's Gospel shows the spirit in which Jesus died. He prayed for His murderers: ' Father, forgive them; for they know not what they do.' " [10]

So we have called the cross the Great Intercessional. It was the final refusal, in the face of the most awful savagery and brutality imaginable, to cut himself adrift from humanity and to despair of its renewal. " He . . . made intercession for the transgressors " in life and in death; and the cross stands in consequence as the final and unmistakable testimony to the fact that God was reconciling the world to himself in Christ.

V

We are thus brought again to the place where atonement has been made. The first-born Son has offered a perfect confession, a sacrifice of obedient self-giving, whereby he affirmed once for all the true nature of man's life as a son of God. By it, in McLeod Campbell's expressive term, he witnessed to man on behalf of God and showed what sonship in God's family really implies. At the same time he has offered a perfect intercession, a sacrifice of loving response to the sin of the brethren, whereby he affirmed, in the face of everything to the contrary, that man could still become a son of God. By it he witnessed to God on behalf of men and mounted up in faith to the vision of man living his true life within the family of God. Thus manwards and Godwards, from within Deity and from within humanity, the Word of the cross has been spoken and reconciliation has been made.[11]

It only remains to consider briefly the appropriation of the Atonement by the sons of men. As we have already suggested, in the field of family relationships there can be nothing in the nature of coercion if the peculiar ethos of these relationships is to be safeguarded. The utterly powerful force is example, not compulsion; action which speaks, not words which paralyze. And where there is estrangement between child and parent, no one can exercise an influence comparable to that of another child within the same family. An outsider cannot interfere; the parent may simply have to wait; but the brother or the sister can say and do things which none other could do. The result of a life of true sonship thus manifested may be the shaming and the humbling and the complete inward change of the one who has been living in resentment and estrangement. He sees the vision of the true relationship between son and father in the words and actions of his brother and he is moved to repentance and change of life, to shame that he has ever doubted and distrusted the father, to an ardent desire to dwell in the relationship of love which is his inalienable right.

So it is with the sacrifice of the Son. There we see one of the human family, loving the Father to the uttermost; loving the brethren to the uttermost. We see real sonship; and we know that we were made to walk in love as dear children and to live as sons of God. We would fain identify ourselves with his Spirit; it exercises upon us a fascination and attraction which we cannot resist. So in identification with him by faith, in receiving him,[12] we become sons of the Father, conformed to the image of the Son of his love. Thus the Atonement is consummated and reconciliation achieves its end.

But not only is the individual brought to the enjoyment of sonship with God; a new family is brought into existence where there is neither Jew nor Gentile, neither bond nor free, neither male nor female, but all are one in Christ Jesus. This is the dominant theme of the most lyrical epistle of the New Testament — The Epistle of Paul to the Ephesians. In Christ, a family was constituted before the beginning of the world to be holy and blameless before God in love; that family was predestinated to receive the full experience of sonship in and through its relationship to Christ and, in due course, in spite of the alienation caused by sin, that experience was made possible ' by the blood of Christ.' For sin had not only caused enmity between men and God; it had produced divisions and antagonisms between man and man, nation and nation. Now, however, through the cross, Christ had reconciled the world to God, and therefore all barriers of race and class were broken down in the common reconciliation. " For he is our peace," he who reconciled both Jew and Gentile to God in one body through the cross. In it the agelong enmity was once for all slain. All were made fellow members of the one household of God.

Thus from our consideration of family relationships we have gained a vision of the perfect Son, living in joyful obedience to the Father's will through all the disciplines and testings of human experience; living too in perfect love towards his fellow men in face of all opposition and persecution; offering finally the supreme sacrifice of obedience and love and thereby bringing into existence a new family, born not of blood, nor of the will of man, but born out of the travail of his own soul on their behalf. In his cross men are reconciled to God and made his sons by adoption; in his cross too men are reconciled to one another and made brothers within the family of God.

" Behold, what manner of love the Father hath bestowed upon us, that we should be called sons of God. . . . Beloved, now are we the sons of God, and it doth not yet appear what we shall be: but we know that, when he [the perfect Son] is manifested, we shall be like him; for we shall see him as he is."

11. The Lamb Slain from the Foundation of the World

"And all that dwell upon the earth shall worship him, whose names are not written in the book of life of the Lamb slain from the foundation of the world." — *Rev. 13:8.*

The phrase which we have chosen as the title of this final chapter is one which has never ceased to fascinate the minds of thoughtful Christians. There is nothing quite like it elsewhere in the New Testament. A certain air of mystery hangs over it, though it seems to suggest at least one thing clearly — that there is a quality of timelessness in the sacrifice of Jesus Christ.

Immediately, however, we are compelled to ask whether this is consistent with the rest of Biblical teaching. Is not the whole emphasis of the New Testament laid on the fact that the cross was an event in history, that it was a once-for-all event, that it was an event which happened at a particular place at a particular time, that it was in very truth the centre of history where one age came to an end and another age began? All this may be admitted without qualification, and yet a place may still be found for the seer's sublime vision " of the Lamb slain from the foundation of the world." For as we have already suggested, if the cross is simply an isolated event in time, without precursor or successor, without context or content, then it is devoid of all meaning for the general life of mankind. Once, however, it is set within the stream of history, it must have connections, however remote, with the source of all history in the mind of God and with the end of all history in the ultimate purpose of God. The Lamb was slain from the foundation of the world; the consummation of all things is the marriage supper of the Lamb. In the midst, on the open plane of history, stands a cross to which was nailed the Lamb of God who takes away the sin of the world.

I

This is a concept of so great importance that we must spend time in seeking to make it somewhat clearer to our minds. We may begin with an illuminating analogy suggested by Dr. Nathaniel Micklem in his book *The Doctrine of Our Redemption*. He is discussing the way in which St. John of Damascus speaks of ' the cross ': at one time he appears to refer to the historic cross, at another to the cross signed on the believer's forehead and at still another to the cross as proclaimed in the Gospel. Yet, Dr. Micklem urges, it is the one cross of our redemption, existing in many modes. For example, he says, " when a house is built, there is first the house in the mind of the architect, second there is the house on the blueprint, third there is the house in bricks and mortar. St. John, if I understand him aright, would say that the house in the architect's mind, the house on the blueprint and the house in bricks and mortar are the same house in three different modes of being." He then applies his illustration and concludes by saying that " the historic event on Calvary, its meaning, its representation in preaching, its ' showing forth ' in sacraments are all modes of one divine action, one event, which we term the Cross."

This is a suggestive analogy and throws some light on the matter which we are considering, but in certain respects it seems to us defective. In the first place, it hardly seems a true parallel to compare the historic cross with the house in the mind of the architect; the utterly distinctive thing about the historic cross is that it stands out clearly upon the open plane of history. Further, when the cross belongs primarily to the

realm of time rather than to that of space, it seems unfortu-
nate to choose the spatial art of building rather than one of
the temporal arts, in order to illustrate the way in which it is
possible to speak of the ' one eternal cross.' While, then, I am
indebted to Dr. Micklem for an illuminating analogy, I cannot consider it fully satisfactory for our purpose. Tentatively
I would offer the following as an alternative illustration.

II

Let us consider the construction of a drama. First the plot
of the drama formulates itself in the author's mind; we need
not seek to enquire how the inspiration comes but often, almost in a flash, the essential sequence of the play becomes vividly clear. Straightway the author grasps it as a unity, not in
the least perfected in detail but complete so far as the basic
movement is concerned. The next stage is the long process of
preparation. The author's thoughts must be set down in black
and white, worked over again and again, shaped and fash-
ioned, until the whole drama is expressed as well as words
can express it. Further, the scenery giving the spatial context,
and the general circumstances giving the temporal context,
must also be provided for. As soon as possible, rehearsals must
be arranged, leading to further corrections and adjustments,
until everything is in readiness for the first public display.
One other matter, however, is bound to occupy a large place
in the author's attention before the first performance can
take place: he must find actors who will understand what
the drama is all about; and, above all, he must find a man to
play the leading part who will have a deep sympathy with his
own mind and a penetrating insight into the real meaning of
the play. When such a man has been found and when he has
been trained and inspired by personal contact with the author

himself, then at last the finished work of art may be presented to the public for the first time.

This, then, is the third stage — the actual performance of the drama at a definite place and at a particular time. There is something peculiarly critical about this first performance. The future influence of the play will very largely depend upon it; if there is success on this occasion, success is likely to continue; if failure, the situation is hardly likely to be retrieved. Assuming, however, that success is achieved, there comes the fourth stage of the continued evolution of the initial idea. This consists in the repetition and reproduction of the drama in many widely varied settings and at widely different periods. Attempts will be made by successive producers to conserve the original but to make it in some way peculiarly relevant to their own day and circumstance. Successive actors too will seek to penetrate more deeply into the spirit of the drama and then to relate it in their own way to their own particular situation. Finally, if there be some prophetic note within the original idea, the time may come when its influence will be so widely felt that the very pattern of society will be moulded to the form of its creative design.

III

Let us now seek to apply our parable to the realm of the purposes and activities of God himself. We begin with the basic thought of the Lamb as it had been slain. How, it may be asked, could this possibly have entered into the mind of God in the midst of original perfection? Our only answer can be that it was a correlate of the very idea of human freedom. If freedom was to be granted to man, the possibility must exist that freedom would be used to resist and despise the Giver of the gift; and if such a possibility could be even conceived, we may believe that God would also conceive a plan for dealing with such a contingency. So, we suggest, the thought of the slain Lamb must have existed as a corollary of the thought of free man: the dramatic sequence of freedom, sacrifice, restoration must, we believe, have been present to the mind of God from the foundation of the world.

With the actual fall of man, the second stage of the cosmic drama begins. The long period of preparation is to take place during which the design of redemption will be more and more clearly expressed in the language of human life. Actors will be chosen and educated, and rehearsals, as it were, will take place within every area of human experience. Is not this a fair description of what is actually shown forth in the Old Testament Scriptures? Within the area of human conflict we see leaders arising such as Moses and Joshua and the Judges and David. These men shared the hardships and disabilities of their fellows but by their own inner integrity and faith and willingness to suffer challenged the oppressor power and led out those who would trust them to a measure of freedom and deliverance. Never did this process attain perfection of form, for there were always imperfections and failures on the part of both leaders and followers. But a rough presentation of the drama was taking place and the way was being prepared for the final production.

Again, within the life of the ordered community there were vivid foreshadowings of the re-establishment of justice through costly suffering. Think, for instance, of the dramatic scene on Mount Sinai when Moses, the lawgiver, realizing the heinousness of the people's rebellion returned unto the Lord and said, " Oh, this people have sinned a great sin, and have made them gods of gold. Yet now, if thou wilt forgive their sin — ; and if not, blot me, I pray thee, out of thy book which thou hast written." Or think of the similar scene at the threshing-floor of Araunah when David, the king and upholder of justice, realizing that judgement was about to fall on the people, pleaded that it might fall only upon himself and his father's house, and insisted upon paying the full cost for the expiation of what was regarded as a national sin. Again, there is nothing like perfection of form, especially in the case of David. But the drama of restoration and restitution was being presented in the rough and an indication given of the movement of the finale.

Yet again, within the cultural life of Israel there are some of the most powerful expressions to be found anywhere in the world's literature of the thought of regeneration and renewal of life coming through suffering and death. There is, for instance, the dramatic Twenty-second Psalm with its vivid portrayal of the man apparently forsaken by God, mocked and despised by his fellows, surrounded by cruel enemies, with his life fast ebbing away; and then the sudden reversal, with paeans of praise and triumph, and the confident cry that as the result of his willing suffering, a seed, a remnant, would be justified and the name of the Lord glorified. Supremely, however, there is the dramatic poem of Isa., ch. 53, with its picture of the suffering servant, despised and rejected of men, apparently stricken and smitten by God, wounded and bruised and at length led as a lamb to the slaughter; but the poem shows that he was suffering for the sins of others and so again there comes vindication out of disaster, life out of death, the uprising of a new seed and its amazing growth in the earth. Here is a wonderful presentation of the drama of regeneration through death and perhaps the nearest approximation which the Old Testament provides to the final form which the drama was ultimately to receive.

Within the family life of Israel the foreshadowings are less obvious. There are glimpses of the divine forgiveness in Joseph's treatment of his brothers, in David's attitude to Absalom and in Hosea's dealing with his wife. But in the Old

Testament the prodigal son is really Israel itself, and the dramatic showing forth of sacrificial love is seen pre-eminently in the patience and long-suffering of God towards the people whom he had chosen for himself. It is no impassible God which the Old Testament sets before us; rather it is a God who in all his dealings with his recalcitrant son reveals that love which was to come to its final outward expression in the climactic drama of the cross.

Having thus dwelt at some length on the second stage of preparation, we need only focus attention for one moment upon the supreme manifestation in history of the sacred drama. At this point our parable inevitably breaks down, for there was a uniqueness, an intensity, a finality in the cross of Calvary such as there could never be in a performance of an earthly drama, however outstanding it might be. Yet at the same time the parable may help us to understand how a complex of actions, envisaged in eternity and partially represented in dramatic events in the life of ancient Israel, came to a full and perfect expression in the suffering and death of the elect Son of God.

IV

We may pursue our parable one stage further and consider the way in which the drama of Calvary has been reproduced and re-enacted in the subsequent life of mankind. Let us, as before, take up the four areas which we have defined and see how the essential movement of the cross may be manifested in the context which each provides.

1. *Heroic Action*. In the earliest period of Christian history this was the field in which the drama of the cross was most often re-enacted. The Church was expanding, encountering opposition and facing danger; at the same time it was aflame with a passion to make the good news of the saving power of

Christ known to all men. In its task of witness, then, it shared his suffering but also triumphed through his victory. *The drama of the cross was reproduced in the life of every missionary who identified himself with the outcast and the oppressed, seeking to lead them out into the freedom of the new life in Christ.*

It would not be hard to give many examples from later history — Ramon Lull, Father Damien, Henry Martyn, David Livingstone. But let us take a striking incident from more recent times. The late Sir George Adam Smith told of how he was once travelling in France on the steamer train between Calais and Paris and how he had as a travelling companion for part of the journey a young priest of the Roman Catholic Church. In conversation he informed Sir George that he was on his way to the Belgian Congo, but before sailing he was going to see his mother, as he said, " for the last time." " But why the last time? " he was asked. " Because," he said, " the average lifetime of a missionary on the Congo is two and a half years." The train was at the station, and as they parted the question was asked, " But — why go? " The young priest placed his hand on his heart and said quietly, " The life that I now live, I live by faith in him who loved me and gave himself for me." In all such heroic lives the drama of the cross is seen afresh.

2. *Vicarious Payment.* With the firm establishment of the Christian community and the consequent changes of emphasis within its life, the field of ordered relationships proved to be the one in which the drama was more often reproduced. As the Church became more settled, problems of the administration of justice within the fellowship were bound to arise. All those who accepted positions of responsibility learned, sooner or later, something of the tension of the cross, for in their task of judicial oversight they were obliged to enforce the rules and disciplines of the community, while in their

rôle as pastors they could not cease to care for those who had gone astray. This tension is particularly evident in the relationships between Paul and the Christians at Corinth. On the one side he feels bound to insist upon order and discipline within the community; on the other side he identifies himself in spirit with those upon whom judgement must fall. *Thus the drama of the cross has been reproduced in the life of every true pastor who has sought to uphold the divine law and yet has identified himself with the ignorant and rebellious, and sought to make retribution vicariously on their behalf.*

A singularly impressive modern-day example is recounted in the last book by C. F. Andrews, published after his death. He tells of a man of good family who had yielded himself up to intemperance and was living a wastrel's life in the slums of East London. The rescue workers tried to help him by sympathy and kindness but it made little impression; then one day the silver vessels for the Communion of the sick were found to be missing. After several weeks, late one night, the man appeared on the doorstep and in an utterly befuddled state produced the vessels from his ragged pocket. Andrews' first impulse had been to take him in again but, having sought for guidance, he decided to do a thing he had never done before — to give the man into custody. Next morning he appeared with the man in court and asked that a light sentence might be given. As a result the man was sent to prison for a month on condition that Andrews would care for him when he was released. So Andrews stood alongside him in his punishment and in his rehabilitation. When, much later, he was asked whether he thought Andrews had done the right thing in taking him to the police station, he answered, " Yes, sir; that was the turning-point of my life; for if you had taken me into the mission house I should have gone straight back to the drink the very next morning." [1] In such an incident we see a submission to justice, coupled with a deep identification with the guilty one; here, surely, is a reproduction of the drama of the cross.

3. *Creative Passion.* A further stage in the Church's life was reached when it became possible for representative men to begin to develop cultural forms: here was another field in which the drama of the cross could be reproduced. For if these chosen men were to be true to the genius of Christianity they could not merely accept traditional forms and material and seek to adapt them to Christian needs. Rather, they must become utterly identified in heart and mind with the central action of their faith and seek to express it in the material which successive ages presented for their use. *Thus the drama of the cross has been reproduced in the life and work of every artist and thinker who has identified himself with the rough and tragic elements of human life and sought to express through them the essential passion of the cross.* In a previous chapter we spoke of the achievements of Bach and Milton in this respect: we might instance many another, as Da Vinci in the realm of painting and Alexander Whyte in the realm of preaching. Let us, however, take a modern example from the realm of historical fiction, where a literary artist gives a deeply impressive rendering of the creative passion of the cross.

The scene is the forest to which Abélard has retired with his faithful servitor Thibault. It is evening, and suddenly they hear a piercing cry: it proves to be a rabbit caught in a trap.

" Thibault held the teeth of the trap apart and Abélard gathered up the little creature in his hands. It lay for a moment breathing quickly, then in some blind recognition of the kindness that had met it at the last, the small head thrust and nestled against his arm, and it died.

" It was that last confiding thrust that broke Abélard's heart. He looked down at the little draggled body, his mouth shaking. ' Thibault,' he said, ' do you think there is a God at all? Whatever has come to me, I earned it. But what did this one do?' Thibault nodded. 'I know,' he said, 'only — I think God is in it too.' . . . 'All this,' he stroked the limp body, 'is because of us. But all the time God suffers. More than we do.' Abélard looked at him, perplexed. . . . 'Thibault, do you mean Calvary?' Thibault shook his head. 'That was only a piece of it — the piece that we saw — in time. Like that.' He pointed to a fallen tree beside them, sawn through the middle. 'That dark ring there, it goes up and down the whole length of the tree. But you only see it where it is cut across. That is what Christ's life was; the bit of God that we saw. . . . We think God is like that for ever because it happened once, with Christ. But not the pain. Not the agony at the last. We think that stopped.' . . . 'Then, Thibault,' Abélard said slowly, 'you think that all this, all the pain of the world, was Christ's cross?' 'God's cross,' said Thibault, 'And it goes on.' 'The Patripassian heresy,' muttered Abélard mechanically. 'But, oh God, if it were true. Thibault, it must be. At least, there is something at the back of it that is true. And if we could find it — it would bring back the whole world.' " [2]

In this tiny drama also the artist has reproduced the very spirit of the cross.

4. *Loving Sacrifice*. A final stage, and yet in another sense a new beginning, came when the Church recognized itself as God's family, bound to him and to each other by ties of mutual love. It was a final stage because no higher conception of the Church could be imagined; at the same time it was a new beginning, for it is of the very essence of family life that there shall be children to take their place in the continuing stream of existence. Within this field there was found still another setting for the reproduction of the drama of the cross. For those who had known love in its richest form — a love which laid down its life for the other members of God's family — could not fail to show forth that love in their relations with those within their own family circle. *Thus the drama of*

*the cross has been reproduced in the life of every parent who
has become identified in love with the wandering and erring
child and has endured the uttermost sacrifice on its behalf.* It
is not easy to set forth examples of this type of re-enaction, for
often it has been in the secrecy and intimacy of the life of the
home. One example, however, may be taken from a modern
writer who, though not speaking directly of his own family,
seems to suggest that it was there that he had seen the one who
would have acted in the way which he proceeds to describe.

" I will ask you to think of a father or, a mother — pure,
holy, tender, loving-hearted — whose own beloved only
child, son or daughter, is branded with the deep reality
of irretrievable disgrace. I will ask you first to compare
the grief of such a mother over the shame of a stranger,
and over the shame of her own, her best-beloved. Even
towards the stranger there might be the deepest concern,
the tenderest, truest, most winning and restorative sympathy. But the shame, which is her own child's, is her
own. *For herself,* the light is gone out of her life. Her
heart is not merely, as in the other case, tenderly concerned. Her heart is broken. . . .
" Yes, it is the mother's heart which is broken for sin;
broken even, it may be, unto death. The child's heart is
less likely to break. The true realization of shame, the
true steady insight into sin, is dulled, not sharpened, by
the indwelling of sin. The heart of the child is not able to
break — at least yet. Only long afterwards, if at all, when
penitence has at last done its slow, penetrating, tranquil-
lizing work, will sin, as sin, be felt and seen as it is. Meanwhile the penitent anguish of the mother who is holy is,
even in proportion to her reality of holiness, more un-
dimmed, keener of edge, deeper in truth, — in the shame
of the child with whom, in nature and in love, she is
wholly self-identified — than it is, than it can be, in the
child of whose mind and will the sin itself is still part." [3]

In sketching this drama in the setting of the home, Dr. Moberly expresses as vividly as anywhere in his great book his
own apprehension of the profound meaning of the cross.

V

The final purpose of all Jesus' parables was to lead men to decision. They were not just attractive stories told to interest and amuse. They were not just clever descriptions of the general structure of human life. They were, indeed, of surpassing interest and possessed a relevance which was universal in its scope. At the same time they were so pointed, so challenging, that men who listened to them were bound to accept or reject — they could not simply remain on neutral ground.

And what is true of the parables of Jesus is, we believe, in some measure true of the parallel which we have sought to outline in this chapter. If the cross expresses the original design and final purpose of God, if it has been expressed at sundry times and in divers manners within the setting of human life, if it has come to a full and perfect manifestation in the death of Jesus on the hill of Calvary, then surely we are confronted by a drama of timeless significance and universal import. No man is outside its range; no man can avoid being confronted by it at some moment in his life. And when the tremendous movement of the drama is being enacted before his eyes, he must accept its implications or he must reject. There can be no neutral ground.

Nowhere have I seen this challenge to decision more powerfully urged than in the concluding section of the first part of Professor Farmer's recent study of the grounds for belief in God. I have been stirred in my own heart by his words, and I should like their impact to be felt by others too.

" The Crucifixion of Jesus confronts the soul of man with a searching dilemma, with the necessity of finally making up his mind. For it means one of two things. Either it means that that sort of believing about God, that sort of living, even when it is at its maximal point of purity and devotion, is so fantastically false, so utterly

wide of the truth, that it cannot stand up to the forces
which actually dominate the world, but is doomed to be
stamped out by them — which is exactly what powerful
leaders and teachers in the world to-day are saying. Or, on
the other hand, it means that it is so true, so firmly rooted
in fact, that it can afford to accept seemingly utter defeat,
knowing that the victory, God's victory, is in the end with
it. One of two things: the Crucifixion of Jesus is either a
great, grim, hoarse, derisive shout of *No* to the proposi-
tion that God is love, gathering into itself and summing
up all those other evil things in human life which seem
also to shout *No* to it; or it is a firm, steady, undefeated
Yes penetrating, persisting through, all these other things.
Who then is to decide which it is? The strange thing is
— though it is not strange in view of the personal nature
of God's dealings with us — the individual man must decide, must answer the question. And if the right answer
be given, it is not the less of the inspiration of God because it is the man's own answer. The conviction that stirs
deep within a man's mind and heart, that he cannot, he
must not, he dare not, join in that grim, hoarse shout of
No is only possible because God has put Christ and the
Cross of Christ into the world, has brought him down the
pathway of his own individual history to a fork in the
road where the challenge of the Cross can no longer be
avoided, has given him a nature capable of discerning, in
its presence, this final dilemma of our personal life —
either to believe in and commit oneself to the God of
Jesus Christ, or to conclude that human existence is *in
fact* what on the surface it most certainly *appears* to be,
namely, in spite of all the incidental fine things that are
in it, a meaningless waste of effort and suffering, ending
in a silence of universal death." [4]

I cannot attempt to add to these impressive words: they serve
to bring the drama right into the immediate present. For although it is of the highest value to have our minds enlightened
and our imaginations quickened by all that we can learn of
the constructing and re-enacting of the sacred drama in the

past, yet nothing can finally take the place of a confrontation by the drama in the present and a resultant determination to make the cross the very substance and pattern of our lives.

VI

And the future? There is no foundation whatever in the New Testament for a lighthearted optimism which sees the world being gradually impregnated with beautiful hopes and noble ideals. It is not a question of the drama becoming gradually outdated, as the kind of situation with which it deals ceases to exist. Rather, is it the faith of the New Testament that the drama will be staged before an ever-widening circle until at length the whole world stands within its range. Then, in the ultimate purpose of God, there will come the final dénouement. From one angle this may be regarded as the final struggle issuing in the victory of the Lamb; from another, as the final judgement issuing in the reign of the Lamb; from another, as the final re-creation issuing in the city of the Lamb; from another, as the final reconciliation issuing in the perfect fellowship of the Lamb. Never shall the drama of the cross be relegated to the realm of the outworn and irrelevant and meaningless; to all eternity it is the Lamb who is to be in the midst of the throne, and his servants shall find their true destiny in worshipping and serving him.

" And he shewed me a pure river of water of life, clear as crystal, proceeding out of the throne of God and of the Lamb.

" In the midst of the street of it, and on either side of the river, was there the tree of life, which barĕ twelve manner of fruits, and yielded her fruit every month: and the leaves of the tree were for the healing of the nations.

" And there shall be no more curse: but the throne of God

and of the Lamb shall be in it; and his servants shall serve him:

" And they shall see his face; and his name shall be in their foreheads.

" And there shall be no night there; and they need no candle, neither light of the sun; for the Lord God giveth them light: and they shall reign for ever and ever." [5]

Notes

1

[1] *The Nineteenth Century and After*, March, 1942, p. 105.
[2] *Out of the People*, pp. 34, 35.
[3] Cf. the even stronger words of Lord Vansittart spoken at a critical period of the war: " Even as Christ suffered for our salvation, every man Jack, every babe Jack in this tried and United Kingdom is suffering to redeem your earth from the Powers of Darkness."
[4] Pages 197, 199.
[5] *The Twilight of France*, p. 379.
[6] Quoted: *The Times Literary Supplement*, Feb. 6, 1943.

2

[1] *The Interpretation of History*, p. 258.
[2] Cf. Luke 1:68 *seq.*; 2:25.
[3] Cf. H. Wheeler Robinson, *Redemption and Revelation*, pp. 232 ff.
[4] *Ibid.*, p. 222.
[5] Vincent Taylor, *The Atonement in New Testament Teaching*, p. 40, footnote.
[6] *Church Quarterly Review* 133, p. 161.
[7] *The Bible Doctrine of Salvation*, p. 56.
[8] E. C. Hoskyns, *The Fourth Gospel* (Vol. II), p. 425.
[9] *Church Quarterly Review* 134, p. 132.
[10] Such a view certainly would not be confirmed by the Fourth Gospel which is at pains to show that Jesus died on the cross at the time when the paschal lamb was being offered and thus took its place. Cf. John 19:36; also I Cor. 5:7, 8.
[11] *Christianity According to St. Paul*, p. 40.
[12] C. A. Anderson Scott, *op..cit.*, p. 35.
[13] I suggest that in the title ' Lamb ' as it is used in John 1:29 and in the Apocalypse we may see the paradox of Shepherd-Lamb coming to a focus. Jesus is both the Lamb who had been slain in the redemption-drama and the Shepherd who leads to living fountains of water.
[14] This *archēgos* is one who " through His resurrection gives the warrant that His followers will share the lot of their heroic deliverer." — Quoted by R. N. Flew, in *Jesus and His Church*, p. 163.

3

[1] Ryder Smith, *op. cit.*, p. 52.
[2] *The Miracle-Stories of the Gospels*, pp. 60, 61.
[3] Cf. Mark 5:30; 7:34.

4 *Jesus and His Sacrifice*, p. 97.

5 *Op. cit.*, pp. 141, 142; cf. p. 190.

6 All these ideas appear in the narrative of the Temptation.

7 *The Intention of Jesus*, p. 143.

8 Cf. A. B. Macaulay, *The Death of Jesus*, Chapter IV.

9 Cf. Vincent Taylor, *Forgiveness and Reconciliation*, pp. 45–47.

10 *Op. cit.*, p. 50.

11 *Op. cit.*, pp. 225, 226.

12 Cf. Vincent Taylor, *The Atonement in New Testament Teaching*, p. 38.

13 James Denney, *The Death of Christ*, pp. 70, 71.

14 *Op. cit.*, p. 73.

4

1 H. Wheeler Robinson, ed., *Record and Revelation*, p. 472.

2 *The Fulness of Sacrifice*, p. 22.

3 This has been powerfully suggested by Dr. H. Wheeler Robinson in various of his writings, but I find it hard to accompany him all the way in his emphasis upon the ' effective realism ' of the prophets' actions.

4 *Jesus and His Sacrifice, passim.*

5 Cf. *The Fourth Gospel*, pp. 596–598.

6 This, we suggest, is the significance of ' brake it.' Part represented the burnt offering dedicated to God alone; part the peace offering shared by the people.

7 The wine, the ' blood of the grape ' (Gen. 49:11; Deut. 32:14).

8 It is possible that the two cups mentioned in the Lucan account were intended originally to represent the two halves of the blood mentioned in Ex., ch. 24.

9 *Op. cit.*, p. 252.

10 The eucharistic teaching of John, ch. 6, is entirely in conformity with these ideas. In his chapter dealing with the sacramental doctrine of the Fourth Gospel, W. F. Howard writes:

" In like manner every member of the Christian Church joined with his fellows in the feast of communion, the outward sign of the fellowship of the Spirit. There they broke the bread and ate of the one loaf, thus symbolizing at the same time the body of Christ given for them in his self-offering for the world, and the unity of the Body of Christ, that is, the whole company of the faithful united in Christ their Head. But the actual death of Jesus was the death of him who had come from above, the Word become flesh. They also drank the wine which represented that life given for the life of the world. Only those who entered by faith into the fellowship of him who really became man and really suffered death upon the cross could share in the spirit now liberated from the body.

' Verily, verily, I say unto you, Except ye eat the flesh of the Son of Man and drink his blood, ye have not life in yourselves. He that eateth my flesh and drinketh my blood hath eternal life . . . he abideth in me and I in him.' " — *Christianity According to St. John*, p. 146.

5

1 Cf. the valuable opening chapter of Dr. O. S. Rankin's book, *Israel's Wisdom Literature*.

2 Rankin, *op. cit.*, p. 36.

3 *Jesus and His Church*, p. 82.

4 The word in the Greek is the same in both cases.

5 There is evidence that Jesus also regarded his newly gathered group as a bride. Cf. Mark 2:20; John 3:27, 29. This band of devotees was a love-gift from the Father and stood in sharp contrast to the unfaithful bride of the Old Testament. Cf. J. Moffatt, *Love in the New Testament*, p. 261. At the same time, it seems to have been much more normal for Jesus to regard them as a family, as children of his own Heavenly Father.

6 This is surely the essential message of the parable of the Prodigal Son.

7 J. W. Bowman, *The Intention of Jesus*, p. 39.

8 This is equally true of the occasions on which Jesus refers to God as ' Father ' or ' my Father.'

9 *Jesus and His Sacrifice*, p. 38.

10 E. C. Hoskyns, *The Fourth Gospel*, p. 67.

11 *Christianity According to St. John*, p. 70.

12 This has been discussed in Chapter 2.

13 James Moffatt, *Grace in the New Testament*, pp. 101, 103.

14 Vincent Taylor, *Forgiveness and Reconciliation*, p. 8.

15 This is done, e.g., by Vincent Taylor, *op. cit.*, pp. 85 ff.

16 The Greek word is slightly different but the root is the same.

17 Quoted by Ryder Smith, *op. cit.*, p. 301.

6

1 After examining certain important passages in the Synoptic Gospels, Dr. Rashdall concludes:

"There is nothing in any of the narratives to suggest that the approaching death was in any way whatever to bring about the forgiveness of sins, or that Jesus was dying ' for ' His followers in any other sense than that in which He had lived for them'— in any sense but that in which other martyrs have died 'for their cause and for their followers. That the death of the Messiah had more significance than the death of other martyrs is true; that the service which in life and death the Messiah was rendering to the world was a greater service than others could render is equally true . . . but the fact remains that there is nothing in the sayings attributed to the Master at the Last Supper which implies any fundamental difference in kind between the service which He was conscious of performing and the service to which He was inviting His disciples " (p. 45). The positive note of self-sacrifice is splendidly emphasized in Dr. Rashdall's writing: what makes his book so disappointing is his insistence that Christianity is just a one-note religion. Unison may have its place in life but most men desire the satisfaction of a rich harmony.

² Dr. Rashdall speaks of the imperative necessity " that we should discuss the question of Christ's own attitude on the matter [i.e., of the atonement] without presuppositions, and without assuming that we are bound to discover in it, even in a rudimentary form, the later doctrine of the Church, or rather any one of the numerous doctrines of the atonement which have at various times been taught as the doctrine of the Church " (p. 5). Presuppositions may be reduced to a minimum and carefully checked: they cannot be eliminated.

³ *The Human Situation*, p. 64.

⁴ *The Religious Function of the Imagination*, p. 8.

⁵ *The Poetic Mind*, pp. 68, 69.

⁶ " We live by symbols. This is because we are all poets in some degree. We are not happy with generalizations and abstractions. We prefer emotion to logic. We count on imagination to carry us through the waste land of the humdrum facts. And we discover, as Aristotle did long ago, that poetry is truer than history. In his autobiography the great Irish poet, Yeats, tells how he *prayed* that his imagination might be rescued from generalization. 'For ten or twelve years,' he says, ' I suffered continual remorse and only became content when my abstractions had composed themselves into picture and dramatization.' " — W. P. Ladd, *Prayer-Book Interleaves*, 36.

⁷ *Op. cit.*, p. 215.

⁸ Before doing this, it may be well to remark that we have no hope of achieving any finality of interpretation in this way. We shall never be able to exhaust the meaning of the cross simply by using the particular thought-forms of any one period. At the same time, we can never escape the challenge to set forth, in metaphors and ideas familiar to our generation, the significance of the great event of Calvary. In the chapters that follow, therefore, we shall endeavour, as far as possible, to use the language and writings of our contemporaries and to appeal, for our comparisons, to situations which confront us in the world of our own day.

7

¹ Christian News-Letter, 148.

² "Struggle of some kind human life will always be on this side of Heaven." — V. A. Demant, in Malvern Conference Report, p. 123. Cf. Edwin Lewis, *A Philosophy of the Christian Revelation*, pp. 295, 296.

³ Commenting on Ex. 7:4, J. Morgan Jones says (*The Revelation of God in the Old Testament*, pp. 70, 71) : "A lively suggestion is in the words 'I will bring forth my hosts.' A general leading his army is the picture. The army of the Lord is Israel and it is brought forth by Him now, and will be led by Him from now onward to fight His battles in the world."

⁴ Milton, "Samson Agonistes," lines 268 *seq*.

⁵ "Life before the death of Christ has touched it is ματαία: i.e., it is futile, it is a groping or fumbling after something it can never find; it gets into no effective contact with reality; it has no abiding fruit. From this subjection to vanity it is redeemed by the blood of Christ. . . . Similarly, life before the death of Christ has touched it is πατροπαράδοτος; it is a kind of tradition or custom, destitute of moral originality or initiative. A man may think he is himself, and that he is acting freely and spontaneously, when he is only indulging self-will, or yielding to impulses of nature in him through which a genuine moral personality has never been able to emerge; but it is the power of Christ's passion descending into the heart which really begets the new creature, to whom moral responsibility — his own — is an original thing, a kind of genius, in virtue of which he does what nobody in the world ever did before, and feels both free and bound to do so." — James Denney, *The Death of Christ*, p. 66.

⁶ William Axling, *Kagawa*, p. 38.

⁷ *Op. cit.*, p. 49.

⁸ *The Healing Cross*, p. 185.

⁹ Cf. E. F. Scott, *The Book of Revelation*, pp. 48, 49.

¹⁰ For an impressive setting forth of the cross as "The Drama of Man's Deliverance" see the final chapter of Edwin Lewis' *A Philosophy of the Christian Revelation*. He writes: "It is incredible that when the truth is so presented it will leave men cold. Men know that life is a struggle. They know that they are opposed by dark and dreadful forces. Even those who accept a mechanistic philosophy cannot escape the feeling that contending powers are all about them and within them. The social field today is shot through with antagonism. Ruthlessness is being embodied in political instruments. The hearts of many are in danger of failing for fear. Rightly understood, the Christian revelation conveys a message of hope to every man who is conscious of the burden and the

mystery, and of what otherwise is but the weary weight of an unintelligible world " (p. 305) .

8

1 *The Hibbert Journal,* July and October, 1942.

2 " Humanity suffers for the sins of humanity, not each individual for his own. Hence vicarious suffering is possible, in so far as the evils which come upon us are due to others' sins. Christ, then, though sinless, in entering into the common life of sinful humanity vicariously suffered for others." — R. S. Franks, *A History of the Doctrine of the Work of Christ,* p. 247.

Cf. too the words of John Donne which gave Hemingway his title: " No man is an *Iland,* intire of it selfe; every man is a peace of the *Continent,* a part of the *maine; . . .* And therefore never send to know for whom the *bell* tolls; it tolls for *thee."*

3 Pages 120, 121.

4 A reviewer in *The Times Literary Supplement.*

5 Cf. Dostoevski, *The Brothers Karamazov,* pp. 341, 342.

6 *The Expositor's Bible* on II Corinthians, pp. 70, 71.

9

1 Pages 43, 44.

2 R. M. MacIver, *Leviathan and the People,* pp. 89, 90.

3 *Along the Indian Road,* p. 232.

4 *Op. cit.,* p. 224.

5 And every time that the bread is broken and the wine outpoured, the normative model of the betrayal night is vividly re-presented before the Church of God.

" It [the Eucharist] embodies the Christian Gospel not in mere words, like a sermon, or in motionless forms, like a mosaic, but like a drama in significant act. We do not simply listen to the story of the Cross, or look at a picture of it. In the bread and wine broken, poured, and offered, we face the reality of Christ crucified." — W. P. Ladd, *op. cit.,* p. 37.

6 Christian News-Letter, 156.

10

1 M. L. Jacks, in *The Spectator,* February 28, 1941.

2 Sidney Dark, *The Church Impotent or Triumphant,* p. 102.

3 Sidney Dark, *ibid.*

4 William McCollum Clow, *The Cross in Christian Experience,* p. 41.

⁵ *Op. cit.,* p. 103.

⁶ *The Fatherhood of God,* pp. 311, 312.

⁷ *Op. cit.,* p. 312.

⁸ Pages 32, 33.

⁹ Kierkegaard employs a telling metaphor, "A son is a mirror in which the father sees himself reflected."

¹⁰ *The Atonement,* pp. 167, 168. Cf. the equally fine passage in James Denney, *The Christian Doctrine of Reconciliation,* p. 251.

¹¹ "Our Lord secures at last the full realisation in human history of the true life which sin destroys. He is the truly Divine, yet perfectly human, reaffirmation of that which sin denies. It is in that reaffirmation — on the part both of God and man — that His redemptive work begins, and by the completion of it that His redemptive work is consummated. All His atoning work is simply founded in and carried to its completion by His persistent reaffirmation, first in spirit and then in doing and suffering, of that true life which sin has contradicted and destroyed. He makes this reaffirmation in those relations of solidarity with the whole race which His relationship to it as its original ground and end involves. He makes it under those conditions of physical nature and of human society which the entrance of sin into the world has brought about — those general conditions by which the righteousness of God has marked the unrighteousness of mankind. He makes it in union with, and through making it is, so to speak, in command of, that Divine Spirit by whom all that He is and does can be reproduced in the race which through that one Spirit is akin to Him. Once let the Son of God, incarnate, completely reaffirm in spirit, character, and conduct the perfection of human life in its Divine relationships, under the penal conditions of mankind, and atonement first and regeneration next are the divinely natural results." — John Scott Lidgett, *The Fatherhood of God,* p. 380.

¹² John 1:12.

11

¹ The story is recounted in C. F. Andrews' *The Sermon on the Mount,* pp. 123–125.

² Helen Waddell, *Peter Abelard.*

³ Robert Campbell Moberly, *Atonement and Personality,* pp. 121–123.

⁴ Herbert H. Farmer, *Towards Belief in God,* pp. 124, 125.

⁵ Rev. 22:1–5.

INDEX